speakout 2ND EDITION

Elementary
Workbook

T0386094

Frances Eales • Steve Oakes • Louis Harrison

CONTENTS

CONTENTS

GRAMMAR

PRESENT SIMPLE: BE

1 Put the words in the correct order to make sentences.

1 A: Yasmin / your / is / name
Is your name Yasmin ?
B: no, / isn't / it. / Anna / name / 's / my
_____ .

2 A: Sofia / are / you
_____ ?
B: David / I / am. / yes, / this / and / is
_____ .

3 A: are / a / student / you
_____ ?
B: I'm / no, / not. / teacher / I'm / a
_____ .
is / teacher, / a / too / David
_____ .

4 A: you, / Sofia and David / to / nice / meet
_____ .
B: nice / you, / meet / to / too
_____ .

2 Complete the conversations with the correct form of *be*.

Conversation 1
Ben: Hello. How are you?
Ed: Er … hello.
Ben: Sorry, [1] *are* you Mr and Mrs Rutter?
Ed: No, we [2]_____. They [3]_____ Mr and Mrs Rutter.
Ben: Oh, sorry.

Conversation 2
Ben: Excuse me. [4]_____ you Jerry Rutter?
Jerry: Yes.
Ben: I [5]_____ Ben Pastor.
Jerry: Oh, hello. Nice to meet you, Ben. This [6]_____ my wife, Sally.
Sally: Hi.
Ben: Sorry. [7]_____ your name Sandy?
Sally: No, it [8]_____. It's Sally.
Ben: Nice to meet you, Sally.

3 Write questions and answers using the prompts.

1 A: you / American? *Are you American?*
B: no / I / Canadian *No, I'm not. I'm Canadian.*
2 A: he / a student? _____
B: no / he / a teacher _____
3 A: we / late? _____
B: no / you / early _____
4 A: they / from India? _____
B: no / they / China _____

VOCABULARY

COUNTRIES AND NATIONALITIES

4 A Find twelve countries in the puzzle.

G	R	E	E	C	E	C	Q	S
P	O	R	T	U	G	A	L	C
R	G	E	R	M	A	N	Y	O
U	S	O	Y	E	Q	A	J	T
S	P	C	U	X	F	D	A	L
S	A	H	V	I	Z	A	P	A
I	I	I	U	C	M	U	A	N
A	N	N	P	O	L	A	N	D
T	H	A	I	L	A	N	D	P

B Write the nationalities for the countries in the puzzle.

_____*Greek*_____   _____
_____   _____
_____   _____
_____   _____
_____   _____
_____   _____

C Write the nationalities from Exercise 4B in the correct column.

1 -an / -ian	2 -ish
German	Polish
3 -ese	**4 other**
Portuguese	Greek

D ▶ 1.1 Listen and underline the stressed syllables in the nationalities in Exercise 4C.

E Listen again and repeat.

READING

5 Read the text and match food 1–6 with countries a)–f).

NATIONAL DISHES AND DRINKS

Where are these fabulous dishes and drinks from?

- ■ Bubble tea, or pearl milk tea is from Taiwan.

- ■ Indonesians eat a rice dish called Nasi Goreng.

- ■ Ful Medames is from Egypt. They make it with beans and lemon.

- ■ Jacket potatoes are from the UK.

- ■ Pide is a food from Turkey. It's Turkish pizza – yum!

- ■ Curry is Indian. It's food cooked in sauce, and it's delicious!

1 Pide	**a)** Indonesia
2 Bubble tea	**b)** Turkey
3 Ful Medames	**c)** India
4 Jacket potatoes	**d)** UK
5 Curry	**e)** Egypt
6 Nasi Goreng	**f)** Taiwan

WRITING

CAPITAL LETTERS

6 Complete the words with the letters in brackets. Use capital letters where necessary.

1 _T_his is a _hoto of _e at the _olosseum in _ome, _taly.
   (t p m c r i)

2 _his is me and my _ustralian _riend, _aul. _e're in _enice.
   (t a f p w v)

3 _his is _enji at a _ar in _adrid. _enji is a _tudent from _apan.
   (t k b m k s j)

4 _ere is _aul again. _e's at _axim's in _aris. _axim's is a _rench _estaurant.
   (h p h m p m f r)

VOCABULARY

OBJECTS

1 A Look at the pictures and complete the crossword.

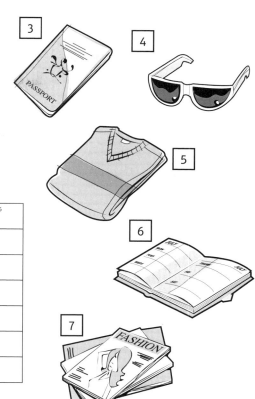

B ▶ 1.2 Listen and write the words from Exercise 1A in the correct column for each stress pattern.

1 O	2 Oo
keys	*passport*

3 Ooo	4 ooO
sunglasses	*mobile phone*

C Listen again and repeat.

LISTENING

2 A ▶ 1.3 Listen to interviews with three passengers at an airport and complete the table.

	Passenger 1	Passenger 2	Passenger 3
Nationality	*German*		
Tourist (T) or on business (B)?		*T*	

B Listen again and tick the things in the passengers' bags.

	Passenger 1	Passenger 2	Passenger 3
laptop			
credit card			
diary			
MP3 player and earphones			
sunglasses			
passport	✓		
camera			
ticket			
newspaper			
magazine			
mobile phone			
keys			

GRAMMAR

THIS/THAT, THESE/THOSE; POSSESSIVES

3 Look at the picture and complete the conversation with *this*, *that*, *these* or *those*.

John:	¹ _These_ are great sunglasses. How much are they?
Shop assistant:	² _____? They're 200 euros.
John:	200 euros!
Shop assistant:	But ³ _____ sunglasses are only twenty euros.
John:	OK. And how much is ⁴ _____ magazine?
Shop assistant:	⁵ _____'s two euros.
John:	Two? OK, here you are.
Shop assistant:	Thanks.

4 A Rewrite the sentences in the plural.

1 That CD's great!
Those CDs are great!

2 This red pen is Anne's.
_____

3 This isn't my key.
_____

4 Where's that ticket?
_____

B Rewrite the sentences in the singular.

1 These books are very good.
_____

2 Those aren't my files.
_____

3 Who are those men over there?
_____

4 Are these your photos?
_____

5 Add one apostrophe (') to each conversation.

1 **A:** Is this your mobile phone?
B: No, it isn't. I think it's Jane's.

2 **A:** Are these DVDs yours?
B: No, they're Suzannas.

3 **A:** Is your friends name Greg?
B: Yes, Greg Hutchens.

4 **A:** Are these Nathans sunglasses?
B: I don't know. Ask him.

5 **A:** Are your teachers photos in the book?
B: Yes, they're on pages 17 and 18.

6 **A:** Where are Irenas tickets?
B: They're on the table.

7 **A:** Is this chocolate cake yours?
B: No, it isn't. It's Lucys.

8 **A:** Are these keys Mr Allisons?
B: Yes, they are.

6 A Rewrite the sentences. Don't repeat the nouns.

1 These glasses are ~~my glasses~~.
These glasses are mine.

2 These keys are your keys.
_____

3 That bag is Jack's bag.
_____

4 Those pencils are my pencils.
_____

5 This mobile phone is Anita's mobile phone.
_____

6 That magazine is your magazine.
_____

B ▶ 1.4 Listen and check.

C Underline the letter *-s* in your answers in Exercise 6A.
1 These glasses are mine.

D What is the pronunciation of *-s* in your answers? Listen again and write /s/ or /z/.
1 These glasses are mine.
 /z/ /s//z/

E Listen again and repeat.

VOCABULARY

TOURIST PLACES

1 A Complete the words. Add the vowels in brackets.
1 snackbar c_ffees_ndwich (add *a* or *o*)
2 t_uristsh_pp_stc_rdb_tterys_uvenir (add *a* or *o*)
3 r_t_rntick_tappl_j_ic_ (add *u* or *e*)
4 tr_ _nst_t_ons_nglet_cketpl_tform (add *a* or *i*)

B Circle the places and things in Exercise 1A.

FUNCTION

MAKING REQUESTS

2 Put the words in the correct order to make requests.
1 have / I / a / coffee, / can / please
Can I have a coffee, please ?
2 Birmingham, / have / I / a / could / return / please / to
_____ ?
3 I / please / batteries, / of / can / those / one / have
_____ ?
4 have / could / sandwich, / I / please / a / cheese
_____ ?
5 I / can / apple juice / have / an / coffee, / and / please / a

_____ ?

3 Complete the conversations with the words in the box.

| ~~do~~ have you that's euro please help can |

Conversation 1
Tourist: Excuse me. ¹___Do___ you speak English?
Shop assistant: Yes. Can I ²_____ you?
Tourist: ³_____ I have these four postcards, please?
Shop assistant: OK. ⁴_____ two euros, please.

Conversation 2
Tourist: Can I ⁵_____ a coffee, ⁶_____?
Waiter: That's one ⁷_____ fifty.
Tourist: Thank ⁸_____.

4 1.5 Listen and tick the speaker (A or B) that sounds more polite.
1 A _____   B ✓
2 A _____   B _____
3 A _____   B _____
4 A _____   B _____
5 A _____   B _____

LEARN TO

LISTEN FOR KEY WORDS

5 A Read the conversations. Underline the two key words in each sentence.
1 A: How much is a <u>coffee</u> <u>cake</u>, please?
   B: It's two euros.
2 A: Could I have a return to Sydney, please?
   B: That's ten fifty.
3 A: Is that a cheese sandwich?
   B: No, it's a chicken sandwich.
4 A: That's eight euros, please.
   B: Ah, I only have six euros.

B ▶ 1.6 Listen and check. Then listen and repeat.

6 A ▶ 1.7 Look at the menu and listen. What do the people order? Write the food and drink for 1–6.
1 ___a tomato salad___   a) € ___2___
2 _____   b) €_____
3 _____   c) €_____
4 _____   d) €_____
5 _____   e) €_____
6 _____   f) €_____

B Listen again and write the prices for a)–f).

* M E N U *

DRINKS
COFFEE | HOT CHOCOLATE | TEA
JUICE | MINERAL WATER

SANDWICHES
EGG | CHICKEN | CHEESE
***
SALADS
GREEN | TOMATO

ICE CREAM

2 LIFESTYLE

VOCABULARY

ACTIVITIES

1 Complete the profile with the verbs in the box.

> do   listen   play   read   watch   go   eat   have

ALLTOGETHER ▲

Personal Profile:

Teresa Alvarez

About Me
I come from Mexico, I'm twenty-three years old and I'm a student. I study politics at UNAM (the National Autonomous University of Mexico). I'm single.

Activities
I ¹ _____do_____ a lot of sport – I ² _____ running every day and I ³ _____ tennis most weeks.

Interests
Going out: I love meeting people and I ⁴ _____ a lot of fun going out with friends.

Food: I like going out to restaurants with friends. We ⁵ _____ Mexican food – tacos are my favourite!

Favourite Music
I ⁶ _____ to different kinds of music, but I really like World Music.

Favourite TV shows
I ⁷ _____ a lot of TV. American programmes like *Breaking Bad* and *The Big Bang Theory* are my favourite.

Favourite Movies
Anything with Johnny Depp!

Favourite Books and Magazines
Vogue! I ⁸ _____ it every month!

2 A ▶ 2.1 Listen and write the words in the box in the correct column for each stress pattern.

> game   newspaper   sport   magazine   coffee   cinema   exercise   MP3 player   DVD   TV   nothing   film   tennis   pasta   fun

1 O	2 Oo	3 oO
game		
4 Ooo	**5 ooO**	**6 ooOoo**
newspaper		

B Listen again and repeat.

GRAMMAR

PRESENT SIMPLE: I/YOU/WE/THEY

3 Look at the information about Francesco and his flatmates, Ben and Tom. Complete Francesco's sentences.

	Francesco	Ben and Tom
watch TV a lot	✓	✗
listen to the radio	✗	✓
eat in fast food restaurants	✗	✗
drink a lot of coffee	✓	✓
read computer magazines	✗	✓
go to the cinema	✗	✓
do sport	✓	✗
play computer games	✓	✓

1 I _____watch_____ TV a lot, but I _don't listen_ to the radio.

2 Ben and Tom _____ TV a lot, but they _____ to the radio.

3 We _____ in fast-food restaurants.

4 We _____ a lot of coffee.

5 Ben and Tom _____ computer magazines.

6 I _____ to the cinema.

7 Ben and Tom _____ sport.

8 We _____ computer games.

4 Write questions and short answers using the prompts.

1 A: you / eat / junk food, Juan?
   Do you eat junk food, Juan?
   B: no / I
   No, I don't.

2 A: you / do / a lot of sport, Kiko?
   B: yes / I

3 A: the students in your class / live / near you?
   B: no / they

4 A: you and Clara / like / pasta?
   B: yes / we

5 A: you / listen to / Radio 5, Dan?
   B: yes / I

6 A: Ursula and Hans / study / English with you?
   B: no / they

7 A: I / have / classes on Sunday?
   B: no / you

8 A: you and your family / eat / together?
   B: yes / we

9 A: Ali and Marco / play / tennis?
   B: yes / they

10 A: you and Ana / drink / coffee?
   B: no / we

LISTENING

5 A Read the course list. Then match the courses with the pictures. Write your answers on the first line.

ADULT EDUCATION COURSE LIST

Digital photography: 9–12p.m.   _____ _____
Salsa for beginners: 7–9p.m.   _____ _____
Singing for fun: 6.30–8.30p.m.   _____ _____
Office yoga: 7.30–9p.m.   _____ _____

B ▶ 2.2 Listen to the conversation. Number the courses in Exercise 5A in the order the people talk about them. Write your answers on the second line.

C Listen again and complete the table.

	Which day?	Where?	What?
Singing for fun	*Monday and Thursday evenings*		
Digital photography		*high school*	
Salsa for beginners			
Office yoga			*stretching and relaxing exercises*

WRITING

AND, BUT, OR

6 Join the sentences. Use one of the words in brackets.

1 On Monday, I leave for work at 9. I get home at 6. (and/or)
   On Monday, I leave for work at 9 and I get home at 6.

2 On Tuesday, I phone my mother. I chat with her for hours. (but/and)

3 On Wednesday, I get up early. I don't go to work – it's my free day. (or/but)

4 On Thursday, I work in the office. I work at home. (but/or)

5 On Friday, I go out late with my friends. I go to bed early. (and/or)

6 On Saturday, I play tennis with Pete at 9. I have lunch with him. (and/but)

7 On Sunday morning, I read a newspaper. It isn't in English! (but/or)

8 On Sunday afternoon, I listen to music. I watch TV. (but/or)

VOCABULARY
DAILY ROUTINES

1 A Put the letters in the correct order to make phrases.

1 eahv fskarbeta   _have breakfast_
2 vhae hlucn   _____
3 og ot dbe   _____
4 teg emho   _____
5 avhe nndire   _____
6 tge pu   _____
7 astrt kowr   _____
8 evale meho   _____
9 nishfi rowk   _____

B Complete the text with the times in the box.

6a.m.   11p.m.   1p.m.   8.a.m.   8p.m.   5p.m.
7a.m.   6p.m.

I get up very early, usually at
¹ ___6a.m.___. Then I have breakfast
at ² _____. I leave home at ³ _____
and go to work. I have lunch at ⁴ _____
and work in the afternoon. I leave work
at ⁵ _____ and get home at ⁶ _____.
At ⁷ _____ it's time for dinner. I go to
bed at ⁸ _____.

GRAMMAR
PRESENT SIMPLE: HE/SHE/IT

2 A Write the he/she/it form of the verbs.

1 sleep   _sleeps_
2 play   _____
3 drink   _____
4 drive   _____
5 relax   _____
6 eat   _____
7 study   _____
8 know   _____
9 wash   _____
10 leave   _____
11 get   _____
12 practise   _____

B Write the verbs from Exercise 2A in the correct column.

1 /s/	2 /z/	3 /ɪz/
sleep<u>s</u>	play<u>s</u>	relax<u>es</u>

C ▶ 2.3 Listen and check. Then listen and repeat.

3 A Complete the text with the present simple form of the verbs in brackets.

Al is a hot dog seller in New York. Every day he
¹ _gets up_ (get up) at 5p.m. and ² _____ (make)
dinner for his two boys – they get home from
school at about 4.30. He ³ _____ (take) the bus
into the city and ⁴ _____ (start) work at 7p.m.
At about 1a.m. he ⁵ _____ (have) two or three
hot dogs for lunch. He ⁶ _____ (work) all night.
At work, he ⁷ _____ (see) a lot of interesting
things and ⁸ _____ (meet) a lot of interesting
people. He ⁹ _____ (finish) work at 3 or 4a.m.
On the bus he ¹⁰ _____ (read) the morning
newspaper. He ¹¹ _____ (get) home at about
6a.m. He ¹² _____ (have) breakfast
with his family and
¹³ _____ (go) to bed
at about 8.30a.m. – and
that's the end of his
day … or night.

B Correct the sentences about Al.

1 Al gets up early in the morning.
   He doesn't get up early in the morning. He gets up
   in the afternoon.
2 Al goes to work by taxi.
   _____ to work by bus.
3 Al has a salad for lunch.
   _____ two or three hot dogs.
4 Al reads a magazine on the bus.
   _____ the morning newspaper.
5 He gets home late at night.
   _____ home early in the morning.
6 Al has lunch with his family.
   _____ breakfast with them.

4 Put the words in the correct order to make questions.

1 live / Eva / does / where
   Where does Eva live ?

2 Juanes / does / coffee / drink
   _____ ?

3 what / 'junk' / does / mean
   _____ ?

4 lunch / he / when / have / does
   _____ ?

5 like / she / does / popcorn
   _____ ?

6 read / does / which / Kay / newspaper
   _____ ?

7 does / how / work / Faisal / come / to
   _____ ?

8 friend / live / does / where / your
   _____ ?

READING

5 A Read the article and answer the questions.

1 Does Al like his job?

2 Does he work at the weekend?

A NIGHT IN THE LIFE OF A HOT DOG SELLER

'In my job I meet a lot of interesting people. People like talking to me. They don't just want a hot dog, they want a conversation. It's great working at night. It's never hot, people are relaxed and they're very hungry. Some nights I sell over 300 hot dogs. I have one customer, Hector – he's a taxi driver; he eats ten hot dogs every night. People ask me, "Al, do you like hot dogs?" Yes, of course I like them. I love them! Hot dogs are *not* junk food; they're good food. My boys love them, too and we have hot dogs for dinner every Saturday night. I don't work at the weekend. I'm with the boys all day and then sleep at night. They play football in the park and I watch them or I play with them. Or I go and get a hot dog!'

B Read the article again. Are the sentences true (T) or false (F)?

1 Al doesn't like people.   *F*

2 People don't talk to Al.   _____

3 People aren't hungry at night.   _____

4 Hector doesn't sell hot dogs.   _____

5 Al doesn't like hot dogs.   _____

6 Al and his boys have hot dogs
    for Saturday dinner.   _____

7 Al sleeps at night at the weekend.   _____

8 Al doesn't go to the park with his boys.   _____

C Correct the false sentences in Exercise 5B.

1   Al likes people.

VOCABULARY

JOBS

6 Look at the pictures and complete the jobs crossword. Then look at the grey boxes. What's the hidden job?

VOCABULARY

THE TIME

1 Write the times in two different ways.

1	7.30	*It's half past seven.*	*It's seven thirty.*
2	9.15	_____	_____
3	11.10	_____	_____
4	2.45	_____	_____
5	5.20	_____	_____
6	8.35	_____	_____
7	10.55	_____	_____
8	1.40	_____	_____

FUNCTION

ASKING FOR INFORMATION

2 A Read the leaflets quickly and look at the gaps. Think about the missing information in each gap.

A

T **TRAIN TIMETABLE**
London to Cambridge

London Kings Cross	¹ *10.52*	11.15
Cambridge	11.54	² _____

B

BANGKOK temple tour

Start time: ³ _____
Finish time: ⁴ _____
Tour start point: ⁵ _____
Adult: ⁶ _____ baht /
    14 euros

C

NATIONAL BANK

Opening hours

Monday–Friday:	⁷ _____ to 4p.m.
Saturday:	10a.m. to ⁸ _____
Sunday:	closed

B Look at the gaps in the leaflets again. Use the prompts to write questions about the missing information.

1 what time / leave?   *What time does the train leave?*
2 when / arrive?   _____
3 what time / start?   _____
4 when / finish?   _____
5 where / start from?   _____
6 how much / cost?   _____
7 what time / open?   _____
8 when / close?   _____

C ▶ 2.4 Listen and check. Then listen and repeat.

D ▶ 2.5 Listen and complete the leaflets in Exercise 2A.

LEARN TO

SHOW YOU DON'T UNDERSTAND

3 A Listen to the conversations in Exercise 2D again. In which conversations do the people show they don't understand?

B Put the words in the correct order to make questions.

1 speak / you / could / slowly, / sorry, / please / more
_____?

2 Wat … / the / me, / excuse
_____?

3 you / that / could / spell
_____?

4 you / could / that / sorry, / repeat
_____?

C Complete the conversations with the questions in Exercise 3B.

1 A: My last name is Weitts.
  B: _____
  A: Yes, that's W-E-I-T-T-S.
2 A: The tour starts at the Wat Mahatat.
  B: _____
  A: Mahatat. The Wat Mahatat.
3 A: How much does the tour cost?
  B: Six hundred and fifty baht.
  A: _____
  B: Oh, sorry: six … hundred … and … fifty … baht.
4 A: How long is the tour?
  B: The tour takes two hours.
  A: _____
  B: The tour takes two hours.

VOCABULARY

FAMILY

1 A Look at the family tree and complete the conversations.

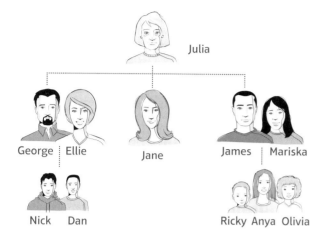

Julia

George Ellie   Jane   James Mariska

Nick Dan   Ricky Anya Olivia

Conversation 1

Jane: Chris, this is my ¹ _mother_, Julia.
Chris: Nice to meet you, Mrs Garnet.
Jane: And this is my ² _____, George, and his ³ _____, Ellie.
Chris: Hello.
Jane: And these are my ⁴ _____, Nick and Dan.
Nick: Hi.

Conversation 2

Chris: Are these your children, Mariska?
Mariska: Oh, let me introduce you. These are my ⁵ _____, Anya and Olivia, and this is my ⁶ _____, Ricky.
Ricky: Hi!
Mariska: And this is James, my ⁷ _____.
Chris: Hello, everyone.

Ricky: And that's my ⁸ _____, George, and my ⁹ _____, Jane.
Chris: Yes, I know. I'm a friend of Jane's.
Ricky: And those are my ¹⁰ _____, Nick and Dan.

Conversation 3

Chris: Ellie, what's that little girl's name? I forget.
Ellie: That's my ¹¹ _____, Anya.
Chris: And her ¹² _____ are Mariska and …?
Ellie: James. We're a big family. A lot of names to remember!

B Look at the underlined letters. Is the pronunciation the same (S) or different (D)?

1	si<u>s</u>ter	mo<u>th</u>er	_S_
2	c<u>ou</u>sin	<u>u</u>ncle	____
3	w<u>i</u>fe	n<u>ie</u>ce	____
4	<u>au</u>nt	f<u>a</u>ther	____
5	s<u>o</u>n	h<u>u</u>sband	____
6	gr<u>a</u>ndfather	p<u>a</u>rents	____
7	da<u>ugh</u>ter	br<u>o</u>ther	____
8	n<u>e</u>phew	fr<u>ie</u>nd	____

C ▶ 3.1 Listen and check. Then listen and repeat.

2 Complete the sentences with family words.

1 My mother's _father_ is my grandfather.
2 My father's _____ is my sister.
3 My sister's _____ are my mother and father.
4 My children's _____ is my sister.
5 My children's _____ is my brother.
6 My mother's _____ is my cousin, Matt.
7 My father's _____ is my cousin, Nina.
8 My father's _____ is my mother.
9 My mother's _____ is my father.
10 My son's _____ are my mother and father.

GRAMMAR
HAVE/HAS GOT

3 A Look at the table and complete the sentences with the correct form of *have got*.

I	a new laptop
my sister	an MP3 player
my brother	an old computer
my parents	a black car
my family	a four-room flat

1 I *'ve got* _____ a new laptop.
2 I _____ an MP3 player.
3 My sister _____ a computer.
4 My parents _____ a car.
5 My brother _____ a computer, but it's old.
6 We _____ a house.
7 We _____ a flat.
8 It _____ four rooms.

B Look at the table in Exercise 3A and complete the questions and short answers.

1 A: ___*Have*___ you ___*got*___ a new laptop?
   B: ___*Yes, I have.*___
2 A: _____ your brother _____ a new computer?
   B: _____
3 A: _____ you _____ a house?
   B: _____
4 A: _____ your sister _____ an MP3 player?
   B: _____
5 A: _____ your flat _____ four rooms?
   B: _____
6 A: _____ your parents _____ a black car?
   B: _____

4 Find and correct five mistakes with *have got* and *be* in each conversation.

Conversation 1
A: I haven't got a pen. ~~Are you~~ one? *Have you got*
B: No, I'm not, but I've got a pencil.
A: Has it got black?
B: No, it's got red.
A: Has it got a rubber?
B: Yes, it is.
A: Can I borrow it? Thanks.

Conversation 2
A: Have you got your camera with you?
B: No, but Fatima's an MP3 player.
A: Has it got a camera, Fatima?
C: No, it isn't. But my mobile phone's got a camera.
A: Has it got good?
C: Not really. It's very small and the pictures haven't got very good.
A: That's OK. Can you take a photo of me?
C: OK, smile! Look. You're a nice smile.

5 Complete the text with the correct form of *have got*.

An only child

It's not unusual to be an only child in the UK. Many families [1] ___*have got*___ only one child. I'm Lucy, I'm an only child and I like it. I [2] _____ a brother or a sister, but that's OK.
I [3] _____ my cousins, my aunts, uncles, grandfathers and grandmothers – and I [4] _____ the noise of a large family; our house is always quiet!
I [5] _____ my own room, too – it's small, but I love it!
My best friend [6] _____ a big family – he [7] _____ three brothers and two sisters! But they [8] _____ a big house, so he shares a room with his two brothers.
[9] _____ I _____ a lot of time with my mum and dad? Yes, I [10] _____. And that time is really special for me.

LISTENING

6 A ▶ 3.2 Listen to two people talking about their families and match the speakers with the phrases. You can use the phrases more than once. There is one extra phrase.

David
Meg

1 hasn't got a job.
2 has got one sister.
3 has got one brother.
4 has got five brothers.
5 has got a good job.

B Listen again. Are the sentences true (T) or false (F)?

1 Tom is Meg's brother. ___T___
2 Meg is close to her sister. ___
3 Nick is David's brother. ___
4 Nick is quite active. ___
5 Jenny is David's mother. ___
6 David and Jenny are close. ___
7 Jenny's husband doesn't like his job. ___
8 Jenny's got three sons. ___

VOCABULARY
PERSONALITY

1 A Add the vowels and write the personality words.

1 knd   *kind*
2 ntllgnt   _____
3 fnny   _____
4 frndly   _____
5 tlktv   _____
6 nknd   _____
7 srs   _____
8 ntrstng   _____
9 stpd   _____
10 qt   _____
11 nfrndly   _____
12 brng   _____

B Write the words from Exercise 1A in the correct column for each stress pattern.

1 O	2 Oo	3 oO
kind		
4 Ooo	**5 oOo**	**6 oOoo**

C ▶ 3.3 Listen and check. Then listen and repeat.

D Complete the conversations with adjectives from Exercise 1A.

1 A: I think Mark's very friendly.
  B: Really? He never talks to me! I think he's very *unfriendly*.
2 A: Andrea's really talkative at breakfast time.
  B: Yeah, I don't like it. I like to be _____ in the mornings!
3 A: Lena's a serious student.
  B: Yes, usually, but she's sometimes very _____.
4 A: The teachers are kind to Greg.
  B: Yes, but some of the children are _____.
5 A: This cat's very stupid!
  B: Don't be horrible! I think she's very _____!
6 A: The first class today is art – that's really interesting.
  B: Yes, but the teacher's _____ – he makes everyone go to sleep!

GRAMMAR
ADVERBS OF FREQUENCY

2 Underline the correct alternative.

1 Mixing yellow and red <u>always</u>/often/sometimes makes orange.
2 The colour red often/sometimes/hardly ever means 'danger' or 'stop'.
3 Apples are sometimes/hardly ever/never purple.
4 In football, the ball is usually/hardly ever/never white.
5 A chef in a restaurant never/sometimes/always has a white hat.
6 Food is often/hardly ever/never blue.
7 Cola is always/sometimes/never brown.
8 People always/often/never drink their coffee white – with milk.
9 Taxis in New York are hardly ever/always/sometimes yellow.
10 Eggs are usually/never/hardly ever white or brown.

3 A Read the emails. Are Sandy and Cristina good flatmates?

> Hi Maria,
>
> How are you? I'm fine, but I've got a new flatmate, Cristina, and she's a real problem. She talks to me never. When she comes home in the evening, I ask her usually about her day. She says, 'Fine!' always and then she watches usually TV or she goes to her room to sometimes sleep! She wants hardly ever to chat. What can I do?
>
> Sandy

> Hi Zsuzsa,
>
> How are you? I'm fine, but my new flatmate, Sandy, is a real problem. She stops talking never. In the evening after classes I'm tired often. I want to usually relax in front of the TV for half an hour or I have sometimes a short rest. She wants always to talk about her day. I have hardly ever the energy to listen.
>
> That's my news. Email me soon!
>
> Cristina

B Read the emails again. Circle the adverbs of frequency and draw a line to show their correct position.

READING

4 A Read the forum post and tick the ideas you agree with.

HELP! forum

| **Question**
Jon,
Ontario | My friend Sam often asks me for money. I usually say no, but sometimes I give him ten or twenty euros. The problem is he never pays me back. I don't want to ask him, but I feel bad about the whole thing. Help! |

Beth writes:	Talk to him about it. Tell him how you feel. You say he's your friend and real friends listen to each other. But remember: money and friends don't mix. Good luck!
Karl writes:	I don't think he's a real friend. It's time to end the friendship – tell him to give you the money and then say goodbye!
Steve writes:	Forget the money. Friends are everything. Money's not important – but don't give him more money!

| **Question**
Patsy,
Christchurch | I work with Joanne and I really like her, but we aren't friends. The problem is that she thinks we're friends. She often asks me to meet her after work and at the weekend. She phones me three or four times a week and she just wants to chat. Help! |

Levente writes:	Maybe it's a good idea to meet her just once at the weekend. You say you like her – well, give her a chance. Good luck!
Miki writes:	That's a problem. Tell Joanne the truth – you're a friendly person, but you aren't her friend!
Cynthia writes:	That's really difficult. Change your telephone number . . . or don't answer the phone. She needs to understand that you don't want to be friends.

B Read the forum post again. Underline two names for each sentence.

1 They're friends.
<u>Sam</u>   Joanne   <u>Jon</u>   Patsy

2 They aren't friends.
Sam   Joanne   Jon   Patsy

3 They say: Don't be friends with him/her.
Beth   Karl   Levente   Miki

4 They say: Tell the truth.
Beth   Steve   Miki   Cynthia

5 They say: Be friends with him/her.
Karl   Steve   Levente   Cynthia

WRITING

DESCRIPTIONS; APOSTROPHE 'S

5 A Complete the text with 's or s.

My friend ¹Jean*'s*_____ got an interesting family. Her brother ²Sam_____ super intelligent and ³he_____ got a good job with a computer company in Sydney. ⁴He_____ married and his ⁵wife_____ name is Grace. ⁶Jean_____ sister ⁷Sally_____ the funny one in the family. She ⁸love_____ telling funny stories and she ⁹work_____ as an actress with the Melbourne Theatre Company. Jean ¹⁰live_____ here in Brisbane in my friend ¹¹Keira_____ apartment. ¹²Jean_____ the 'baby' of the family. ¹³She_____ got a big heart. People always say that ¹⁴she_____ very kind.

B Match 1–14 in Exercise 5A with meanings a)–d). What does 's/s mean?

a) is
b) has   *1,*
c) possessive
d) *he/she/it* form of verb

C Read the texts. Put in nine missing apostrophes (').

My teacher's called Pilar. Shes a language teacher – she teaches Spanish. Pilars classes are always very interesting. She works very hard to make her students speak to each other. We do lots of fun activities like quizzes and working in pairs. Pilars really interested in us and because of this we are interested in her. Our teachers got an award for her work: best Spanish teacher of the year!

I know Mark from playing games online. He loves games and he plays all the time – hes a really good player. Hes very quick. Marks family is quite small – hes got one sister and she also plays online games all the time. Sometimes I think they see each other online more than at home!

D Write about a person you know well. Write 45–65 words. Use the texts in Exercise 5C to help you.

VOCABULARY
TIME EXPRESSIONS

1 A Look at the table and complete the sentences about Tara.

My week	Sun	Mon	Tue	Wed	Thu	Fri	Sat
sleep late							✓
do sport		✓		✓		✓	
have lunch at home		✓			✓		
clean the flat	the first and third Friday of every month						
go shopping	✓	✓	✓	✓	✓	✓	✓
meet friends for dinner							✓
go to the cinema	one or two times every year						
phone Mum	✓✓	✓✓	✓✓	✓✓	✓✓	✓✓	✓✓

1 Tara _sleeps_ late _once a week_ .
2 She _____ sport _____.
3 She _____ lunch at home _____.
4 She _____ the flat _____.
5 She _____ shopping _____.
6 She _____ friends for dinner _____.
7 She _____ to the cinema _____.
8 She _____ her mother _____.

B Find and correct six mistakes with time expressions in the text.

I live in Los Angeles and I like going to the beach and surfing. I go to Malibu beach once a week, usually on Saturday. At the weekend I meet friends and we go to the cinema or a café, or go to a club. We go to the cinema three or four times the year and go to a club once time a month. We meet in cafés two times week and call each other on every day. Because I'm usually very busy, I only clean my flat on first Sunday of every month.

FUNCTION
MAKING ARRANGEMENTS

2 A Complete the conversation with the words in the box.

Are you free   is good for you   would you like
Do you like   How about   sounds good   don't like

A: Hi, Stefanie. ¹_Are you free_ tomorrow?
B: Yes, I am. What ²_____ to do?
A: I'm not sure, really. ³_____ going to a club?
B: Mmm … I ⁴_____ loud music.
A: ⁵_____ films?
B: Yes, I do.
A: OK, let's go and see the new James Bond film.
B: Where is it showing?
A: At the ABC in town. It's on twice a day.
B: What time ⁶_____? Afternoon or evening?
A: Evening, I think.
B: OK, ⁷_____. See you there!

B Complete the conversations. Write one word in each gap.

1 **A:** What _would_ you like to do tonight?
   B: How _____ going to the cinema?
2 **A:** Are you _____ on Saturday?
   B: Yes, I am. Would you _____ to go shopping?
3 **A:** So, what _____'s good for you?
   B: Well, I finish work at six, so _____ about meeting at seven?
4 **A:** Do you want to see *Hotel Budapest* tonight?
   B: Yes, _____ is it showing?
   A: At the Odeon. It's on at seven.
   B: Hmm … that's a _____. I finish work at seven.

LEARN TO
SHOW INTEREST

3 Complete the words.

1 **A:** We've got a new baby! A little girl!
   B: That's fa_ntastic_! What's her name?
2 **A:** I always go swimming before I go to work.
   B: That's gr_____. It's very good for you.
3 **A:** My sister isn't here. She isn't very well.
   B: Oh. That's a sh_____. I hope she's OK soon.
4 **A:** We never go on holiday. We haven't got any money.
   B: That's aw_____! Everyone needs a holiday.
5 **A:** Oh no! the airport's closed and I've got a flight this afternoon.
   B: That's te_____! Why is it closed?
6 **A:** I've got a new girlfriend. She's beautiful *and* intelligent.
   B: That's wo_____! Where's she from?

VOCABULARY REVIEW

1 A Add the vowels in each group.

1	
f i n i sh	V
sw _ _ t _ r	O
c _ m _ r _	_____
P _ l _ nd	_____
_ r _ sh	_____
w _ _ t _ r	_____

2	
n _ wsp _ p _ r	_____
h _ _ rdr _ ss _ r	_____
l _ s t _ n t _	_____
cr _ d _ t c _ rd	_____
C _ n _ d _	_____
M _ x _ c _ n	_____

3	
C _ l _ mb _ _	_____
_ mbr _ ll _	_____
_ cc _ _ nt _ nt	_____
d _ _ n _ th _ ng	_____
_ d _ pt _ r	_____
K _ r _ _ n	_____

4	
_ ng _ n _ _ r	_____
s _ _ v _ n _ r	_____
g _ t _ b _ d	_____
V _ _ tn _ m	_____
m _ g _ z _ n _	_____
P _ rt _ g _ _ s _	_____

B In each group find: a job (J), two objects (O), a country (C) a nationality (N) and a verb or verb phrase (V).

C Match stress patterns a)–d) with groups 1–4 in Exercise 1A.

a) ooO   _____4_____

b) Oo   _____

c) oOo   _____

d) Ooo   _____

D ▶ R1.1 Listen and repeat.

GRAMMAR PRESENT SIMPLE

2 A Complete the text with the present simple form of the verbs in brackets.

IS THIS A REAL JOB? MEET ROY, THE HOLIDAY VOLUNTEER

Roy [1]'s _____ (be) Canadian and [2] _____ (work) in a youth hostel in Corfu, Greece. He and the other hostel workers [3] _____ (be) volunteers – they [4] _____ (not get) money for their work. Every day Roy [5] _____ (get up) at six and [6] _____ (have) breakfast in the hostel. He [7] _____ (not cook) the meals. Cynthia [8] _____ (be) the chef and she [9] _____ (do) all the shopping and cooking. Every morning, Roy [10] _____ (clean) the rooms and [11] _____ (help) on the organic farm at the hostel, growing food for the guests. In the afternoons, he [12] _____ (not work) and he usually [13] _____ (go) to the beach. After dinner, he and the hostel guests often [14] _____ (chat) together. 'It [15] _____ (be) a great job,' Roy says. 'Everyone's very friendly. I [16] _____ (not want) the summer to end.'

B Write questions using the prompts.

1 how old / be / Roy?   *How old is Roy?* _____
2 where / be / he / from? _____
3 where / be / the hostel? _____
4 how much / money / the volunteers / get? _____
5 when / Roy / get up? _____
6 who / be / Cynthia? _____
7 she / clean / the rooms? _____
8 what / Roy / usually / do / in the afternoons? _____
9 what / he and the guests / do / in the evenings? _____
10 he / like / his job? _____

C Answer the questions in Exercise 2B.

1 *He's twenty-seven.* _____
2 _____
3 _____
4 _____
5 _____
6 _____
7 _____
8 _____
9 _____
10 _____

VOCABULARY PERSONALITY

3 A Put the letters in order and write the words to complete the riddles.

1 I never talk, but I'm not very ___quiet___ (tqeiu).
2 I'm not _____ (eeIlnintgit), but I always know the time.
3 I'm usually quite _____ (sisoreu), but not very _____ (nikd) or _____ (leirnyfd).
4 I'm really _____ (lavttikea) and I never listen.
5 I'm quite _____ (pidsut), but I write in many languages.

B Match objects a)–e) with riddles 1–5 in Exercise 3A.

a) a radio   ___4___
b) a watch   _____
c) a dog   _____
d) a pen   _____
e) the TV news   _____

GRAMMAR HAVE/HAS GOT

4 Complete the sentences with the correct form of *be* or *have got*. What's the answer to question 8?

1 My name ___'s___ Amari.
2 I _____ one brother and one sister.
3 My mother _____ one sister.
4 She _____ (not) any brothers.
5 My mother's sister _____ Jen.
6 Jen _____ Henry's wife.
7 Jen and Henry _____ two nephews and one niece.
8 _____ I a boy or a girl?

VOCABULARY/FUNCTION REVISION

5 A Complete the poems.

Poem 1
I ¹do*n't* _____ like my mobile ²ph_____.
I ³of_____ want to be alone.
But then my ⁴m_____ phone, it rings.
I really do not ⁵l_____ these ⁶th_____!

Poem 2
'What ¹t_____ does the train ²le_____, please?'
'At ³h_____ past four. Here, take ⁴th_____.'
'Two single ⁵ti_____? Are they for me?'
'Yes, for five ⁶eu_____ – they're not for free!'

Poem 3
¹'Co_____ I have a sandwich, ²pl_____?'
'Of ³co_____, what kind? Meat or ⁴ch_____?'
'Oh, I'm not sure, so ⁵ca_____ I please
have one of those and one of ⁶th_____?'

Poem 4
'Are you free at half ¹p_____ five?'
No, ²so_____, that's when my friends arrive.'
'Then ³ho_____ ⁴ab_____ meeting at three?'
'Sorry, I'm ⁵bu_____.' 'When are you ⁶fr_____?'

B ▶ R1.2 Listen and check. Then listen and repeat.

LISTENING

6 A ▶ R1.3 Listen to a conversation at a hotel reception. Circle the correct picture for the lost item.

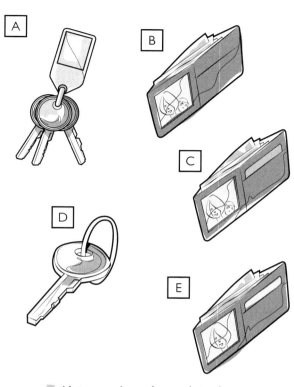

A   B   C   D   E

B Listen again and complete the report.

AIRPORT HOTEL

LOST AND FOUND PROPERTY REPORT

Receptionist: _Angela West_ _____

Guest: ¹_____

Room number: ²_____

Mobile phone number: ³_____

Item lost:

⁴_____ with ⁵$ _____,

⁶_____ card and ⁷_____

Item checked and returned: ☐

Signature: _V Moretti_

Date: ⁸_____

CHECK

Circle the correct option to complete the sentences.

1 A: Are _____ your keys on that table?
B: No, I think they're Franco's.
a) those **b)** these **c)** this

2 When _____ work?
a) you finish **b)** you do finish **c)** do you finish

3 A: Are you from Canada?
B: No, I'm _____.
a) Mexicish **b)** Mexican **c)** Mexico

4 My parents _____ on Fridays.
a) go often out **b)** often go out **c)** go out often

5 A: What's the time?
B: It's _____.
a) a quarter eleven **b)** half to five **c)** eight fifteen

6 David's a _____ child. He never smiles.
a) serious **b)** funny **c)** unfriendly

7 A: Is your name Chung?
B: Yes, _____.
a) I am **b)** it is **c)** my name is

8 A: Can you help us?
B: Sorry, I _____ time.
a) haven't got **b)** don't have got **c)** hasn't got

9 A: What do you do in the evenings?
B: I go to the cinema _____ I do nothing.
a) or **b)** and **c)** but

10 A: What's that?
B: It's a birthday card for my _____.
He's four today.
a) niece **b)** uncle **c)** nephew

11 _____ at the health centre?
a) Jason does work **b)** Does Jason work
c) Works Jason

12 A: Is Carlos married?
B: _____
a) No, he not. **b)** No, he isn't. **c)** He's no married.

13 My _____ is in the office.
a) dairy **b)** diery **c)** diary

14 _____ a sandwich, please?
a) Can I have **b)** Could I **c)** Do I have

15 Eva _____ her MP3 player everywhere.
a) listens to **b)** listen to **c)** listens

16 A: Susan, _____ is Julio.
B: Hi, Susan. Nice to meet you.
a) this **b)** he **c)** here

17 Paolo _____ dogs.
a) no likes **b)** don't like **c)** doesn't like

18 How about _____ to the cinema?
a) go **b)** going **c)** we go

19 They _____ a lot of sport.
a) do **b)** make **c)** take

20 Ricardo _____ twenty-five.
a) is **b)** has got **c)** have

21 A: Where are Kris and Marta?
B: _____ in the café.
a) There **b)** Their **c)** They're

22 You're very _____ today. Are you OK?
a) quite **b)** quiet **c)** happy

23 A: Is this your pen?
B: No, I think it's _____.
a) Elena **b)** Elena's **c)** mine

24 A: How often do you go to a concert?
B: _____
a) One a month. **b)** One in a month.
c) Once a month.

25 A: Do you like films?
B: _____
a) Yes, I like. **b)** No, I don't like. **c)** Yes, I do.

26 I'm not Sylvie's father, I'm her brother!
She's my _____!
a) daughter **b)** aunt **c)** sister

27 Michelle, _____ free tonight?
a) are you **b)** do you **c)** you are

28 I _____ go to the cinema – maybe once a year.
a) never **b)** hardly ever **c)** sometimes

29 _____ a computer?
a) Has Ian got **b)** Ian has got **c)** Has got Ian

30 That isn't your book. It's _____.
a) my **b)** Ana **c)** mine

RESULT /30

VOCABULARY
ROOMS AND FURNITURE

1 A Find ten rooms and furniture words in the puzzle.

L	I	V	I	N	G	R	O	O	M	Z
C	W	L	N	O	I	N	A	G	E	R
U	A	K	I	T	C	H	E	N	M	I
P	R	Q	U	G	B	A	T	E	R	O
B	D	I	S	H	E	L	V	E	S	T
O	R	E	Y	B	D	E	A	T	O	H
A	O	Z	R	M	R	U	K	P	F	E
R	B	A	L	C	O	N	Y	Q	A	V
D	E	A	T	C	O	D	E	S	K	T
P	O	E	A	R	M	C	H	A	I	R

B Write the words from the puzzle in the correct column.

Places in a house	Furniture
living room	

GRAMMAR
THERE IS/ARE

2 A Read the advert and complete the conversation with the correct form of *there is/are*.

ROOM FOR RENT

One bedroom for rent in a large flat with other students

Good location – only ten minutes from the station

Rent: €400 per month

Phone: Eduardo on 0427 392 28409

A: Hi, Eduardo, my name's Ken. I'm interested in the flat. Can I ask you some questions?
B: Sure.
A: ¹ ___Is there___ a living room?
B: No, ² _____, but ³ _____ a big kitchen. We use it as a living room.
A: And ⁴ _____ a television?
B: We've got a small TV in the kitchen and ⁵ _____ an internet connection in each room.
A: Oh, that's good. So at the moment, how many people ⁶ _____ in the flat?
B: ⁷ _____ two of us – me and Karol. Karol's Polish and I'm from Argentina. ⁸ _____ anything else you want to know?
A: Er … oh yes, are you near the shops?

B: Well, ⁹ _____ about five or six shops near the station and ¹⁰ _____ a large shopping centre about ten minutes away.
A: OK, thanks. It sounds great!

B Say the sentences. Then underline the stressed word in each sentence.
1 Is there a <u>living</u> room?
2 There's a big kitchen.
3 Is there a television?
4 How many people are there?
5 There are two of us.
6 There's a large shopping centre.

C ▶ 4.1 Listen and check. Then listen and repeat.

VOCABULARY
PREPOSITIONS

3 Underline the correct alternative.
1 A: Where's Antonia?
   B: She's *on/<u>in</u>/behind* her bedroom.
2 A: I want to take a photo of everyone.
   B: OK. Samad, could you stand *on/under/ in front of* Tomas?
3 A: Where's your flat?
   B: It's *on/between/above* that shop.
4 A: Is there a café near here?
   B: Yes, there's one *between/on/in* the cinema and the post office.
5 A: Have you got today's newspaper?
   B: Yes. it's *in/on/between* the kitchen table.
6 A: OK, let's go.
   B: No, wait. Always look *behind/above/next to* you when you start your car.
7 A: Who's that *next to/between/in* your dad in the photo?
   B: That's my brother, Stefano.
8 A: Where's the cat?
   B: Look *under/above/between* the sofa.

1 _mirror_
2
3
4
5

READING

4 A Match the words in the box with 1–5 in the photo.

lamp ~~mirror~~ curtain sofa picture

B What do you think? Underline the alternative that you think is correct.

In a small room …

1 *have/don't have* lots of small furniture.
2 *use/don't use* one or two pieces of large furniture.
3 *have/don't have* a lot of pictures.
4 *put/don't put* a mirror on the wall.
5 *open/don't open* curtains in the day.
6 *paint/don't paint* your walls a dark colour.

C Read the text and check your answers.

D Look at the photo in Exercise 4A. Complete the sentence with *There's/There are*.

1 _There are_ no armchairs.
2 _____ a big sofa next to the window.
3 _____ two pictures behind the shelf.
4 _____ a curtain.
5 _____ a big mirror on the wall.
6 _____ a lamp in the room.
7 _____ a rug on the floor.
8 _____ no cups on the table.
9 _____ no cupboards.
10 _____ a shelf between the sofa and the wall.

TOP TIPS FOR SMALL ROOMS
BY INTERIOR DESIGNER MARIA WRIGHT

In a small home it's important to choose the right furniture. With the wrong furniture, your room can look crowded but with the right furniture, it can look spacious* and large.

People with small rooms usually make a big mistake: they put lots of furniture in the room. They often have two or three small armchairs and tables or a table and a desk – and they put lots of small pictures on the walls.

A small room looks good with one or two big pieces of furniture, for example a sofa or a table, for relaxing, eating and working. Have one or two pictures – no more – and put up a mirror. A mirror in the right place gives more light and makes the room look big. Windows are very important because they make a room look light and spacious. Use curtains but don't close them in the day. Put wallpaper on one wall and paint the other walls a light colour, for example white or yellow; don't use brown or black or other dark colours.

*spacious = has a lot of space

WRITING

COMMAS

5 A Read the text and put in six commas.

A man lives on the twelfth floor of a tall building. Every morning he leaves home, locks the door takes the lift down to the lobby opens the front door and leaves the building. In the evening he gets into the lift presses a button goes to the tenth floor opens the lift doors and walks up the stairs to his flat. Sometimes there's someone else in the lift and he goes up to the twelfth floor.

B What do you think? Why does the man only go to the tenth floor in the evening, when he lives on the twelfth floor?

LISTENING

1 A ▶ 4.2 Listen to a tour guide and number the street names in the order you hear them. Which four does he *not* talk about?

a) Wood Street _____
b) King William Street _____
c) St Martin's Le-Grand _1_
d) Cheapside _____
e) Fore Street _____
f) Honey Lane _____
g) London Wall _____
h) Prince's Street _____
i) Bread Street _____
j) Moorgate _____
k) Milk Street _____
l) Threadneedle Street _____

B Listen again and match the places with the things you can do there.

1 Museum of London _e_
2 the Barbican _____
3 Moorgate _____
4 the Monument _____, _____

a) send a postcard
b) see all of London
c) see a film or a play
d) get something to eat
e) see very old jewellery

VOCABULARY

PLACES IN TOWNS

2 Where do you go when …? Complete the crossword.

Across row 1: S U P E R M A R K E T

Across
1 You need some food for the weekend.
5 You want to watch a play.
6 You want to borrow a book.
7 You want to watch a film.
9 You like doing exercise.
10 You want to buy a stamp and send a letter.

Down
2 You want to see some beautiful paintings.
3 You need some aspirin.
4 You want to speak to a police officer.
8 You like looking at very old objects.

GRAMMAR

CAN FOR POSSIBILITY

3 Complete the conversations with the correct form of *can* and the words in brackets.

a) A: Excuse me, [1] _can I buy_ (I / buy) stamps here?
B: Yes, [2] _____ (you). But [3] _____ (you / not / send) your postcard, sorry. You need to go to the post office.
b) A: [4] _____ (my son / play) tennis here?
B: No, [5] _____ (he). But there's a sports centre in West Street – [6] _____ (he / play) there.
c) A: Where [7] _____ (we / find) presents for our friends?
B: [8] _____ (you / go) to that shop over there.
d) A: [9] _____ (we / get) tickets here?
B: Yes, [10] _____ (you).
A: And [11] _____ (we / pay) by credit card?
B: No, sorry, [12] _____ (you).

4 A Complete the quiz questions. Use *where*, *can* and the verbs in the box.

> eat   watch   travel   speak   see

WHERE IN THE WORLD ...?

1 *Where can you eat* mooncake?
   a) Mexico   b) China   c) Sweden

2 _____ four languages in one country?
   a) Switzerland   b) Canada   c) Japan

3 _____ Michelangelo's famous statue of David?
   a) Brazil   b) Spain   c) Italy

4 _____ across eleven time zones in one country?
   a) Russia   b) the USA   c) India

5 _____ sixteen different football teams in one city?
   a) Madrid   b) London   c) Rio de Janeiro

B Do the quiz.

C Read the sentences and check your answers to the quiz.

1 Mooncake is a very sweet cake. You eat it in China, at the Mid-Autumn Festival.
2 In Canada you hear two languages: French and English; but in Switzerland there are four official languages: Italian, French, German and Romansch.
3 The statue of David is in Italy. You visit it in Florence.
4 India has got one time zone, the USA has got four and in Russia you go through eleven time zones.
5 Rio and Madrid have got a lot of football teams, but in London you choose between sixteen different football clubs. Arsenal, Chelsea and West Ham United are some of them.

D Add *can* to the sentences in Exercise 4C.

1 Mooncake is a very sweet cake. You can eat it in China, at the Mid-Autumn Festival.

VOCABULARY

PREPOSITIONS

5 A Read the sentences and look at the picture. Write the names of the basketball players.

1 Eduardo is in front of Dirk.
2 Andrei is opposite Eduardo.
3 Steve is on the right of Dirk.
4 Theo is behind Steve.
5 Tony is next to Andrei.
6 Neně is on the left of Tony.
7 Jorge is opposite Neně.

A *Dirk*
B _____
C _____
D _____
E _____
F _____
G _____
H _____

B Look at the picture again. Underline the correct alternative.

1 Andrei is *on the left of/on the right of* Tony.
2 Steve is *in front of/opposite* Theo.
3 Neně is *opposite/behind* Jorge.
4 Tony is *behind/next to* Neně.
5 Eduardo is *next to/on the left of* Jorge.
6 Andrei, Neně and Tony are *opposite/near* each other.

VOCABULARY
THINGS TO BUY

1 A Write the shop names under pictures 1–10.

1 _____sports shop_____

2 _____

3 _____

4 _____

5 _____

6 _____

7 _____

8 _____

9 _____

10 _____

B Complete the things you can buy from the shops in Exercise 1A.

1 Go to shop 1 to buy tra*iners__* or a swi_____ cos_____.
2 In shop 3 you can buy new_____ and mag_____.
3 You can buy jea_____ and a jac_____ in shop 4.
4 Do you want to buy a music C_____ or a film D_____ ? Go to shop 5.
5 You can buy sh_____ and med_____ in shop 9.
6 You go to shop 7 when you need a SIM c_____, hea_____ or a mem_____ sti_____.

FUNCTION
SHOPPING

2 Add the words in the box to the conversations.

~~you~~ 'll can in too got problem them enough 're it expensive they

Conversation 1

you
A: Can ⋀ help me?
B: Yes?
A: Have you got these jeans black?
B: Black? I think so. Yes.
A: Oh, they aren't big. Have you got in size 16?
B: Er … let me look. Ah, yes.
A: Great, I take them. How much are?
B: They £39.99.

Conversation 2

A: I help you?
B: Yes, we need a Scotland football shirt for Duncan.
A: OK. Try this one.
B: No, it's big. Have you it in small?
A: Here you are.
B: Thanks. That's great. How much is?
A: £60.
B: What? £60! That's too.
C: Mum!
B: No. No, thank you. Sorry, Duncan.
A: Fine. No.

LEARN TO
SAY NO POLITELY IN A SHOP

3 Put the words in the correct order to complete the conversation.

Assistant: help / I / can / you
¹*Can I help you*_____?

Customer: thanks / looking, / just / I'm
²_____.

you / have / small / in / this / T-shirt / got
³_____?

Assistant: no, / medium / only / sorry. / in
⁴_____.

Customer: no, / isn't / right. / it / anyway / thanks
⁵_____.

Assistant: red / we've / in / it / got
⁶_____.

Customer: not / mmm, I'm / think / I / sure. / to / need / it / about
⁷_____.

5 FOOD

VOCABULARY
FOOD AND DRINK

1 A Complete the words.

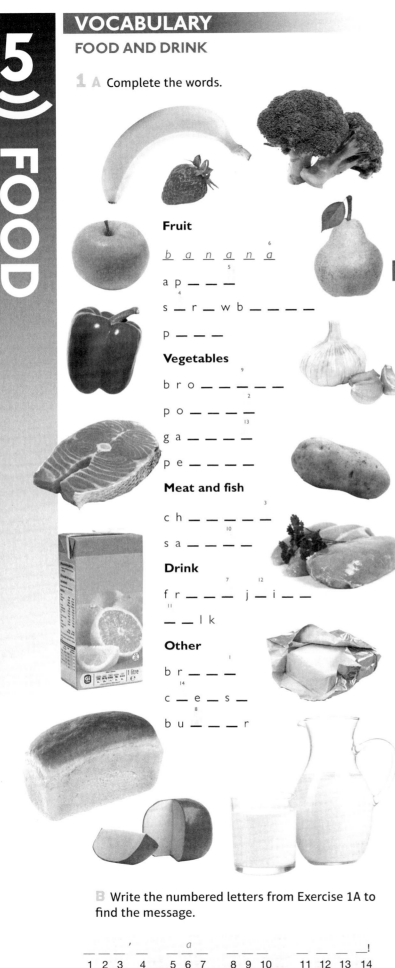

Fruit

_b_ _a_ _n_ _a_ _n_ _a_ ⁶

a p _ _ _ _ ⁵

s _ r _ w b _ _ _ _ _

p _ _ _ ⁴

Vegetables

b r o _ _ _ _ _ ⁹

p o _ _ _ _ _ ²

g a _ _ _ _ _ ¹³

p e _ _ _ _ _

Meat and fish

c h _ _ _ _ _ _ ³

s a _ _ _ _ _ ¹⁰

Drink

f r _ _ _ ⁷ j _ i _ _ ¹²

_ _ l k ¹¹

Other

b r _ _ _ _ ¹

c _ _ e _ s _ ¹⁴

b u _ _ _ r ⁸

B Write the numbered letters from Exercise 1A to find the message.

_ _ _ ' _ _ _ _ _a_ _ _ _ _ _ _ _ _ _ _ !

1 2 3   4   5 6 7   8 9 10   11 12 13 14

2 A Look at the underlined letters. Is the pronunciation the same (S) or different (D)?

1	mi̱lk	chi̱cken	_S_
2	fi̱sh	garli̱c	_____
3	sa̱lad	a̱pple	_____
4	pe̱pper	che̱ese	_____
5	o̱nions	no̱odles	_____
6	bana̱na	gra̱pes	_____
7	lettu̱ce	bu̱tter	_____
8	ju̱ice	fru̱it	_____

B ▶ 5.1 Listen and check. Then listen and repeat.

GRAMMAR
COUNTABLE AND UNCOUNTABLE NOUNS

3 A Underline the correct alternative.
1 I drink _milk_/milks every day.
2 My parents eat a lot of _fruit/fruits_.
3 We often have _egg/eggs_ for breakfast.
4 I don't like _pea/peas_.
5 I don't eat _meat/meats_.
6 I really hate _rice/rices_.
7 We hardly ever have _bean/beans_.
8 There's a lot of _pasta/pastas_ in my cupboard.

B Make the sentences in Exercise 3A true for you.
1 _____
2 _____
3 _____
4 _____
5 _____
6 _____
7 _____
8 _____

4 Write sentences using the prompts. Make the nouns plural where necessary.
1 apple / good / for you
   Apples are good for you.
2 coffee / good / for you?
   _____
3 there / a lot of / sugar / the cupboard
   _____
4 there / a lot of / tomato / the fridge
   _____
5 he / like / grape?
   _____
6 I / not like / butter
   _____
7 you / eat / a lot of / biscuit?
   _____
8 we / not eat / a lot of / ice cream
   _____

READING

5 A Read the article and match recipes 1–3 with shopping lists A–C.

TOO BUSY TO EAT?

Do you have a busy lifestyle? When you come home from work, are you too tired to cook in the evenings? Here are three easy-to-make dishes from TV chef James Conway.

1 Eggs à la Provençale

A dish with a sophisticated name but in fact, it's very simple. Mix together three eggs, some tomato sauce, a small onion and some salt and pepper. Put some oil in a frying pan and when it's hot, add the egg mixture. Stir it around. There you go!

2 Pasta salad

This is a flexible dish, so you can eat it every day. Mix together some cooked pasta – I like three-colour pasta – and two types of cooked vegetables (e.g. broccoli, tomatoes, corn on the cob, green peppers). Add some oil and chilli sauce, stir it around … and enjoy!

3 Cola chicken

Cola chicken is simple to make. You need a chicken, some cola, an onion and a green pepper. Cut up the chicken, the onion and the green pepper and put them together in a pan. Add some cola, some herbs and spices and cover with aluminium foil. Bake at 350 degrees for one hour.

A
pasta (three-colour)
tomatoes
broccoli
chilli sauce
oil

B
eggs
tomato sauce
one onion
salt
oil

C
chicken
cola
green pepper
herbs and spices

B Which two shopping lists are not complete? Read the recipes again and add the missing ingredients to the lists.

GRAMMAR

NOUNS WITH A/AN, SOME, ANY

6 Complete the sentences with *a/an*, *some* or *any*.

1 Pasta salad hasn't got ___any___ meat in it, but it's got _____ vegetables.
2 **A:** Are there _____ vegetables in Cola chicken?
   B: Yes, it's got _____ onion and _____ green pepper.
3 There isn't _____ chilli sauce in Eggs à la Provençale, but there's _____ tomato sauce.
4 Two dishes have got _____ oil in them and one hasn't got _____ .
5 **A:** Is there _____ salt and pepper in the pasta salad?
   B: No there isn't, but there's _____ hot sauce.
6 Cola chicken is _____ very simple dish.

7 Write sentences with *there's/there are* and *some/any*.

1 ✓ fruit ✗ vegetables
   There's some fruit, but there aren't any vegetables.
2 ✓ bread ✗ butter
   _____
   _____
3 ✗ fruit juice ✓ water
   _____
   _____
4 ✗ bananas ✓ apples
   _____
   _____
5 ✓ grapes ✗ cheese
   _____
   _____
6 ✓ pasta ✗ rice
   _____
   _____
7 ✗ onions ✓ carrots
   _____
   _____
8 ✓ salt ✗ pepper
   _____
   _____

VOCABULARY
CONTAINERS

1 Vic and Bob are going on a camping trip. Complete their conversation with the words in the box. Make them plural if necessary. There are two extra words.

can bottle bag cup packet jar bowl carton mug

Bob: OK, Vic. Is everything here?

Vic: Yes, I think so.

Bob: OK. Three [1] _cans_ of baked beans?

Vic: Yes.

Bob: And have we got [2] _____ to eat the beans out of?

Vic: Er, yes.

Bob: Five [3] _____ of water?

Vic: Right.

Bob: Please tell me we've got some [4] _____ of orange juice – you know you forget things.

Vic: Yes, we've got two of them.

Bob: A [5] _____ of cigarettes?

Vic: Bob, this is a no smoking holiday!

Bob: OK, OK. A [6] _____ of jam?

Vic: Yes.

Bob: Ten [7] _____ of sweets?

Vic: Bob, you're on a diet!

Bob: But they're sugar-free sweets.

Vic: Huh!

Bob: Two rolls of toilet paper?

Vic: Er, toilet paper? Oh no!

GRAMMAR
HOW MUCH/MANY; QUANTIFIERS

2 A Write questions using *how much/many* and a word/phrase from each column. Make the nouns in column A plural if necessary.

A	B
1 child	is there in a hamburger?
2 letter	are there in English?
3 beef	is there in a 25-metre swimming pool?
4 vowel	are there in the English alphabet?
5 cent	is there in one can of cola?
6 water	are there in the average American family?
7 juice	are there in a euro?
8 sugar	is there in ten kilos of oranges?

1 *How many children are there in the average American family?*

2 _____

3 _____

4 _____

5 _____

6 _____

7 _____

8 _____

B Match answers a)–h) with questions 1–8 in Exercise 2A.

a) 100 _____5_____

b) 375,000 litres _____

c) two _____

d) 40 grams _____

e) twenty-six _____

f) five _____

g) about 3.5 litres _____

h) 114 grams – one kilo makes eight burgers _____

3 Make sentence b) the opposite of sentence a). Use the quantifiers in the box.

quite a lot of   a lot of   much   many   none   no

1 a) I don't drink very much coffee.

   b) I drink _quite a lot of_ coffee.

2 a) I've got a lot of friends.

   b) I haven't got _____ friends.

3 a) There's a lot of pasta in the jar.

   b) There isn't _____ pasta in the jar.

4 a) I haven't got much time to relax.

   b) I've got _____ time to relax.

5 a) There are some tomatoes in the fridge.

   b) There are _____ tomatoes in the fridge.

6 a) Stamps? Yes, there are some here.

   b) Stamps? No, there are _____ here.

4 Find and correct ten mistakes with quantifiers in the conversations.

1 A: How ~~many~~ milk do we need? *much*
   B: Two cartons.
2 A: Is there any orange juice in the fridge?
   B: No, not many – just one carton.
3 A: How much biscuits do you eat in a week?
   B: Quite a many. I love biscuits!
4 A: There's none water in this bottle. It's empty.
   B: That's OK. There's another bottle in my bag.
5 A: Are there any tomatoes in the fridge?
   B: Not much – two or three.
6 A: How many money have you got?
   B: Quite lot!
7 A: How many bananas are there in that bowl?
   B: No one – it's empty.
8 A: Have we got much ice cream?
   B: Yes, we've got a quite lot.

LISTENING

5 A ▶ 5.2 Listen to a radio programme and choose the correct answer.

On the Junk Food Lover's Diet …
a) you can eat a lot of junk food.
b) you can eat a little junk food.
c) you can't eat any junk food.

B Complete the questions with *how much/many*.

1 _How many_ hamburgers can you eat in a week?
2 _____ chocolate milk can you drink in a week?
3 _____ pieces of pizza can you eat in a week?
4 _____ packets of biscuits can you eat in a week?
5 _____ ice cream can you eat in a week?
6 _____ cola can you drink in a week?

C Listen again and answer the questions in Exercise 5B.

1 half

WRITING

PARAGRAPHS

6 A Read the blog and number the topics in the order the writer writes about them. Which two topics does the writer not give information about?

a) drinks _____
b) snacks _____
c) fast food _____
d) breakfast ___1___
e) foreign food _____
f) dinner _____
g) lunch _____

EATING IN IZMIR

I'm from Izmir in Turkey and my family loves food. From breakfast to dinner, we always eat fresh food. Breakfast is simple: eggs, cheese, bread and tomatoes. We sometimes eat cooked eggs with Turkish sausage – that's really good. We don't usually have cereal with milk for breakfast like they do in the UK – there are lots of other delicious things to eat!

I have lunch with my husband when he can come home from work; the children have lunch at school. We usually have a light lunch – soup and bread, or rice and chicken. Something easy to get is pide – Turkish pizza; we eat it with salad. And we often have a yoghurt drink called Ayran with our pide or some milk. My favourite pide is cheese with egg on top.

Our main meal is dinner. All the family comes to eat and sometimes we have other family members too – cousins, aunts, uncles. We eat around eight o'clock. We start with cold food – different small dishes made from vegetables. Our main meal is usually meat or fish with rice and salad. Then we have fruit or something sweet.

With all that food, eating dinner can take a long time! But we love chatting and telling each other about our day.

B Write four or five paragraphs about how your family eats. Write 80–100 words.

VOCABULARY
RESTAURANT WORDS

1 Complete the article with the words in the box. Use each word twice.

> menu   chef   dishes   bill   ~~order~~   tip   waiter

The American diner

The American diner is a great place to eat, but it's strange for foreigners. When you sit down, someone brings you a glass of ice water. You don't [1] _order_ the water – it just comes. The [2] _____ is not a simple list of food. It's a long list with hundreds of [3] _____. A [4] _____ in a diner can cook anything and everything! Luckily, there are often pictures of some of the [5] _____ in the [6] _____ to help you choose. When you [7] _____ a simple sandwich, the [8] _____ asks you lots of questions – what sort of bread, if you want cheese on it, etc. He writes all the information down and gives it to the [9] _____. At the end of the meal, you ask for the [10] _____. Usually, you leave the money on the table with the [11] _____ and you leave a [12] _____ of 15–20 percent. It's important to leave a [13] _____ – in the USA, a [14] _____ doesn't get much money!

FUNCTION
ORDERING IN A RESTAURANT

2 A Put the words in the correct order to make a conversation.

Waiter: ready / you / order / to / are
[1] _Are you ready to order_ ?

Customer: soup, / like / I'd / onion / please / some
[2] _____ .

Waiter: like / a / you / would / course / main
[3] _____ ?

Customer: some / could / lamb / I / roast / have
[4] _____ ?

Waiter: you / would / like / what / vegetables
[5] _____ ?

Customer: I / and / have / please / potatoes / peas, / can
[6] _____ ?

Waiter: drink / something / to
[7] _____ ?

Customer: I / some / mineral / have / could / water
[8] _____ ?

B Complete the conversation with sentences a)–f).

a) No, thanks.
b) Eat in, please.
c) Can I have two chicken sandwiches, please?
d) Can I have a cola and a water?
e) No, medium fries, please.
f) A large cola, please.

Server: Afternoon. What can I get you?
Customer: [1] _c_
Server: Certainly – two chicken sandwiches. Large fries with those?
Customer: [2] _____
Server: What drink would you like with your meal?
Customer: [3] _____
Server: Sure. Small, medium or large cola?
Customer: [4] _____
Server: Anything else?
Customer: [5] _____
Server: Is that eat in or take away?
Customer: [6] _____
Server: Thanks. Have a nice meal.

LEARN TO
UNDERSTAND FAST SPEECH

3 A ▶ 5.3 Listen and tick what the customers order.

	Customer 1	Customer 2	Customer 3
hamburger	✓		
chicken sandwich			
fries			
lettuce			
onion			
tomato			
corn on the cob			
salad			

B Read at the phrases from Exercise 3A. Draw lines to show the linking.

1 a hamburger with‿onion‿and tomato
2 could I have a chicken sandwich
3 corn on the cob
4 onions on the sandwich
5 lettuce and onion
6 and a salad too, please

GRAMMAR
WAS/WERE

1 Complete the sentences with the correct form of *was/were*.

1 Jan and I ___were___ in Paris at the weekend.
It ___was___ expensive, but interesting.
2 Simon and his wife _____ (not) at the theatre yesterday.
They _____ at the cinema.
3 I _____ late, but the teacher _____ (not) angry.
4 Louise _____ sorry that you _____ (not) at her party.
5 We _____ in New York last summer and the people _____ very friendly.
6 The film _____ (not) funny, but the popcorn _____ really good!

2 Write questions and short answers using the prompts.

1 Paul Newman / actor? ✓ Canadian? ✗
   a) *Was Paul Newman an actor?*   *Yes, he was.*
   b) *Was he Canadian?*   *No, he wasn't.*
2 Beatrix Potter / writer? ✓ English? ✓
   a) _____ _____
   b) _____ _____
3 Beethoven and Wagner / dancers? ✗ German? ✓
   a) _____ _____
   b) _____ _____
4 Confucius / doctor? ✗ Chinese? ✓
   a) _____ _____
   b) _____ _____
5 Che Guevara and Eva Perón / singers? ✗ Argentinian? ✓
   a) _____ _____
   b) _____ _____

3 Complete the sentences with the correct present simple or past simple form of *be*.

1 Jan___'s___ quite talkative now, but he ___wasn't___ (not) very talkative when he was a child.
2 There _____ a lot of people in the office yesterday afternoon, but there _____ only one person here now.
3 The weather _____ (not) very nice last weekend, but it _____ beautiful now.
4 My mother _____ retired now, but for most of her life she _____ a teacher.
5 We _____ (not) at home yesterday, but we _____ here today.
6 The food here _____ fine last week, but this meal _____ (not) very good.
7 I _____ (not) very well yesterday and I _____ (not) well today.
8 Svetlana _____ at school with me when we were children and now she _____ a famous politician.
9 There _____ a lot of people at the concert last night, but there _____ (not) many here tonight.
10 I can see you _____ (not) very happy today. What's the matter? You _____ OK yesterday.

VOCABULARY
DATES AND TIME PHRASES

4 A Write the dates.

1 19/3/1959 *March the nineteenth, nineteen fifty-nine /*
the nineteenth of March, nineteen fifty-nine
2 1/5/2010 _____ /
_____
3 31/3/2002 _____ /
_____
4 30/10/1995 _____ /
_____
5 26/1/2005 _____ /
_____
6 13/10/1957 _____ /
_____
7 21/5/1910 _____ /
_____
8 6/1/1805 _____ /
_____

B ▶ 6.1 Cover your answers in Exercise 4A. Listen and tick the dates you hear. Which one do you *not* hear?

5 Add *on, in, ago, yesterday* or *last* to each sentence. Sometimes two answers are possible.

on/last
1 It was very cold ⁄ Friday.
2 I was at university 1995.
3 He wasn't at home a week.
4 We were at the party weekend.
5 Were you at work Wednesday?
6 My parents were both eighty years old year.
7 The children were tired morning and today, too.
8 It was cold July.
9 We were in the café afternoon.
10 Simon was here ten minutes, but he isn't here now.

READING

6 A Read the article and tick the best title.

1 WORK AND FRIENDSHIP DON'T MIX   2 FILM STAR ROMANCES   3 FAMOUS FRIENDS

Britney and Justin, Kate and Leonardo … celebrities who have something in common: a close friendship.

Some film stars were friends when they were children. Americans Leonardo DiCaprio and Tobey Maguire (*Spider-man*) were good friends, starting when they were child actors looking for work on the same films and TV shows.

Work often brings famous people together. Justin Timberlake and Britney Spears were on the *Mickey Mouse Club Show*, a children's TV programme, together when they were eleven years old. George Clooney and Brad Pitt were co-stars in *Ocean's Eleven* and are very close now.

Sometimes friends in real life play lovers on screen and that can be difficult. Kate Winslet and Leonardo DiCaprio are good friends, but they don't have a romantic relationship. In the film *Titanic*, for both of them, the kissing scenes were strange. 'It was like I was kissing my brother,' says Kate.

Of course, there are stars who don't want to be friends with other stars. Hugh Grant says he doesn't like spending time with other actors. 'I don't have any actor friends,' Grant says. 'I'm friends on the film and then I walk away.'

B Read the article again. How do the stars know each other? Are they friends from childhood (C), friends from work (W), or does the article not say (?)? Tick the correct boxes. Sometimes two answers are possible.

	C	W	?
Leonardo and Tobey	✓		
Justin and Britney			
George and Brad			
Kate and Leonardo			

C Read the article again. Are the sentences true (T) or false (F)?

1 Leonardo and Tobey were on the same TV show together. _____F_____
2 George and Brad are good friends. _____
3 Kate and Leonardo had a romantic relationship in real life. _____
4 Kate doesn't think it was easy to be in a romantic film with Leonardo. _____
5 Hugh Grant has got a lot of actor friends. _____
6 He's unfriendly when he works with other actors. _____

D Complete the sentences with the words in the box. Then read the article again and check.

away   with   together   on   for (x2)   in (x4)

1 The celebrities in the article all have something ____in____ common.
2 Leonardo and Tobey were child actors looking _____ work on the same films.
3 Work brings famous people _____.
4 George Clooney and Brad Pitt were co-stars _____ *Ocean's Eleven*.
5 Sometimes friends _____ real life play lovers on screen.
6 The kissing scenes _____ the film *Titanic* were strange _____ both Kate and Leonardo.
7 Hugh Grant doesn't want to be friends _____ other stars.
8 He says he's friends _____ the film and then he walks _____.

GRAMMAR
PAST SIMPLE

1 A Complete the life story of Anita Roddick. Use the past simple form of the verbs in the box.

| grow up leave open (x2) die meet travel sell |
| come have go work study get |

Anita Roddick started The Body Shop, the first 'green' cosmetics* company. She was born Anita Perelli in the UK in 1942 and ¹___grew up___ in Littlehampton in the south of England.
Her parents ²_____ from Italy and she ³_____ three brothers and sisters.
After she ⁴_____ school, Anita ⁵_____ to Bath College and ⁶_____ to become a teacher. After college, she ⁷_____ all around the world. Then she ⁸_____ Gordon Roddick and they ⁹_____ married in 1970. Anita and Gordon ¹⁰_____ a restaurant and then a hotel.
At the same time Anita ¹¹_____ for the United Nations.
She ¹²_____ the first Body Shop in Brighton, England, in 1976. The shop ¹³_____ only fifteen items with only natural ingredients. It now sells over 300 items to 77 million customers and in 2004 was the twenty-eighth top name in the world of business. Anita Roddick ¹⁴_____ in 2007. She left behind a husband and two daughters.

*cosmetics = make-up, for example lipstick, mascara, hand cream

B Correct the sentences about Anita Roddick.
1 Anita lived in Italy.
  She didn't live in Italy.
2 She went to Bath University.
  _____
3 She became a teacher.
  _____
4 After college she stayed at home.
  _____
5 She and her husband started a café.
  _____
6 She had a son.
  _____

2 A How do you pronounce *-ed* in past simple verbs? Write the past simple form of the verbs in the box in the correct column.

| ~~work~~ change love play finish start stop |
| want help try enjoy travel hate |

1 /t/	2 /d/	3 /ɪd/
worked		

B ▶ 6.2 Listen and check. Then listen and repeat.

C Write the past simple form of the verbs.

1	think	*thought*	7	know	_____
2	meet	_____	8	draw	_____
3	speak	_____	9	write	_____
4	grow	_____	10	sleep	_____
5	wake	_____	11	leave	_____
6	teach	_____	12	buy	_____

D ▶ 6.3 Listen to the vowel sounds in the verbs in Exercise 2C. Write them in the correct column.

1 /ɔː/	2 /e/
thought	
3 /əʊ/	**4 /uː/**

3 Write questions about Anita Roddick.
1 Where *did her parents come from*_____?
  Her parents came from Italy.
2 Where _____?
  She grew up in Littlehampton.
3 How many _____?
  She had three brothers and sisters.
4 What _____?
  After school, she went to Bath College.
5 When _____?
  She got married in 1970.
6 Where _____?
  She opened the first Body Shop in Brighton.
7 When _____?
  She died in 2007.

LISTENING

4 A Read the texts. Then look at the table below.
Are the sentences true (T) or do the texts not say (?)? Tick the correct boxes.

I'm Zsilan. I was born in Beijing. My birthday is 8th May. Because my real parents died, an Australian man and woman adopted* me, so now they are my mummy and daddy. Now I live in Sydney.

*adopt = take into a new family

Zsilan   Lin

My name is Lin. My birthday is 8th May.
I was born in Beijing, but I don't remember my real parents. Because I have Australian parents now, I live in Melbourne.

	T	?
1 Zsilan and Lin are from China.		
2 They were born in the same year.		
3 Their Australian parents adopted* them.		
4 They know each other.		

B ▶ 6.4 Listen and check. Are the sentences you marked *?* in Exercise 4A true?

C Listen again and underline the correct answer.
1 Philip and Denise brought Zsilan home when she was about *one/two*.
2 At first, Zsilan was very *happy/unhappy*.
3 Philip and Denise put *Zsilan's letter/Zsilan's photo* on the website.
4 Zsilan and Lin looked *the same/different*.
5 The girls *lived/didn't live* together.
6 Philip and Denise had the tests *one year/two years* ago.

VOCABULARY
LIFE STORY COLLOCATIONS

5 Complete the story with the verbs in the box.

| ~~went~~   met   worked   got   became   started |

Adam's parents moved from Romania to New Zealand when he was very young. Adam ¹___went___ to school in Auckland. He was very happy there and studied medicine at University. He ²_____ a doctor and ³_____ in a hospital. At the hospital, he ⁴_____ Irina, another doctor, also from Romania. They ⁵_____ married and stayed in New Zealand. Last year they ⁶_____ a website for Romanians living in New Zealand.

WRITING
BECAUSE AND SO

6 Join each pair of sentences with *because* or *so*. Write the story.
1 Kasia didn't study last night. She felt too tired.
2 She needed some fresh air. She went out for a walk.
3 It was a warm evening. There were a lot of people in the street.
4 She met an old friend and they wanted to talk about old times. They went to a café.
5 They stayed there for hours. They had a lot to talk about.
6 Then they went to a restaurant. They were both very hungry.
7 Kasia's friend had a car. He drove her home at the end of the evening.
8 They wanted to meet again. He gave her his phone number.
9 Kasia tried the number but it didn't work. Kasia isn't very happy now!

Kasia didn't study last night because she felt too tired.
She needed some fresh air … _____

_____
_____
_____
_____
_____
_____
_____
_____
_____
_____
_____
_____

VOCABULARY

ACTIVITIES

1 Complete the sentences with the verbs in the box.

> wrote   did   went (x2)   saw   read   stayed (x2)

1 Yesterday was really cold, so I _stayed_ at home. I_____ my homework, watched TV and _____ an email to my cousin in Berlin.

2 We _____ shopping on Saturday – I spent all my money!

3 I _____ for a walk in the morning and then, in the afternoon, I _____ my friends.

4 Emma was tired, so she _____ in bed and _____ her book.

FUNCTION

ASKING FOLLOW-UP QUESTIONS

2 A Put the words in the correct order to make questions.

1 weekend / how / your / was
How was your weekend _____?

2 did / do / what / you
_____?

3 did / what / see / film / you
_____?

4 good / it / was
_____?

5 with / go / you / who / did
_____?

6 on / you / did / what / do / Sunday
_____?

7 you / did / go / where
_____?

8 music / was / how / the
_____?

9 did / get / you / time / what / back
_____?

10 now / tired / you / are
_____?

B Match answers a)–j) with questions 1–10 in Exercise 2A.

a) With my cousin, Ian.   _5_

b) Great! The bands were fantastic!   _____

c) Well, on Saturday we went to the cinema.   _____

d) Perfect!   _____

e) The new Batman film.   _____

f) To Hyde Park, in London.   _____

g) On Sunday I went to a rock festival with Fran.   _____

h) Yes, very good.   _____

i) No, I feel fine.   _____

j) After midnight.   _____

LEARN TO

EXTEND CONVERSATIONS

3 A Circle the best answer to show interest.

1 A: What did you do on Saturday?
B: I had lunch with my grandparents.
A: **a)** It was nice.
   (b) That sounds nice.

2 A: Did you have a good day yesterday?
B: No, we went for a walk and it rained!
A: **a)** Really? That sounds interesting.
   b) So what did you do?

3 A: Did you have a good weekend?
B: I wasn't very well, so I stayed in bed.
A: **a)** That sounds awful!
   b) It was terrible!

4 A: How was your weekend?
B: Fantastic, thanks!
A: **a)** Why, what did you do?
   b) Really? It was fantastic!

5 A: Did you do anything special at the weekend?
B: No, we just stayed at home and relaxed.
A: **a)** That sounds terrible.
   b) That sounds lovely.

B ▶ 6.5 Listen and check. Then listen and read aloud at the same time.

4 Complete the conversation with phrases a)–i).

A: Hi, Jamala. How was your weekend?
B: OK, thanks.
A: Did you go to Gerhardt's jazz concert?
B: Yes, I did. [1] _h_
A: Really? [2] _____?
B: Well, no, there weren't … [3] _____
A: That sounds bad! [4] _____.
B: Gerhardt's mother and father, but [5] _____
A: That's good. [6] _____
B: No, I didn't. [7] _____
A: That's quite early. [8] _____
B: He was happy. [9] _____

a) they enjoyed it.

b) Did you get home late?

c) Who were the other people?

d) How did Gerhardt feel about it?

e) only me and two other people.

f) The concert ended at about ten o'clock.

g) Were there many people there?

h) ~~It was very good.~~

i) He loves playing, so it wasn't a problem for him.

GRAMMAR PAST SIMPLE

1 A Complete the forum posts with the past simple form of the verbs in the box.

> be (x5) bring buy (x2) do eat go (x2)
> have (x2) play see

DO YOU REMEMBER THE 60S?

DORIS K Well, we ¹ _were_ a typical family. We ² _____ (not) poor. We ³ _____ the same kind of furniture as now. In the living room there ⁴ _____ armchairs, a sofa and a black and white television. We ⁵ _____ our first colour TV in 1968.

TERRY G We ⁶ _____ (not) food at the supermarket – every morning a man ⁷ _____ fresh milk, bread and eggs to our house.

JOHN M After school, my friends and I ⁸ _____ to the big supermarket next to the post office. For ten pence we got five big bars of chocolate and ⁹ _____ it all!

ELOISE B There was so much new technology – there ¹⁰ _____ new machines in the kitchen and the garden, and new styles of cars. Of course, we ¹¹ _____ (not) mobile phones, laptops or tablets! Life ¹² _____ was nice and slow.

WINSTON T When I think of the 1960s I think of family. We always ¹³ _____ things together. We were a big family with three of us boys and five girls. At the weekend we ¹⁴ _____ football or other games and we often ¹⁵ _____ for walks. Sometimes we went to the theatre in town and ¹⁶ _____ a play. The important thing was that we were together.

B Write questions using the prompts.

1 Doris and her family / poor?
Were Doris and her family poor?

2 when / her family / buy / their first colour TV?
_____

3 Terry's family / go shopping for food / at the supermarket?
_____

4 where / they / buy / milk / bread / eggs?
_____

5 how much / chocolate / John and his friends / get / for ten pence?
_____

6 Winston / go out / with friends / at the weekend?
_____

C Answer the questions in Exercise 1B.

1 _No, they weren't._
2 _____
3 _____
4 _____
5 _____
6 _____

VOCABULARY REVIEW

2 A Look at the forum posts in Exercise 1A and find:

1 two rooms in a house
living room, _____
_____

2 two pieces of furniture
_____
_____

3 four electronic items
_____
_____

4 four weekend activities
_____
_____

5 three places in town
_____
_____

B Put the letters in the correct order to make words and phrases. Start with the underlined letters.

a) iigdnn mroo _dining room_
b) pobacurd _____
c) epcoil tisotan _____
d) remmoy ckits _____
e) deeshaphon _____
f) yats ni deb _____
g) bedrawor _____
h) og nshioppg _____
i) ummsue _____
j) trabomoh _____

C Add the words in Exercise 2B to the groups in Exercise 2A.

3 Find twelve food words in the puzzle.

C	H	O	C	O	L	A	T	E
H	B	V	U	L	T	E	A	B
I	I	L	G	R	A	P	E	U
C	S	Y	O	G	H	U	R	T
K	C	M	X	C	R	B	B	T
E	U	I	V	D	Y	R	E	E
N	I	L	V	Z	L	E	A	R
Q	T	K	B	A	N	A	N	A
H	O	N	E	Y	M	D	N	N

GRAMMAR   COUNTABLE AND UNCOUNTABLE NOUNS

4 A Add -s where necessary in the food on the list.

2 kilos of oranges	1 tin of bean
1 kilo of apple	2 packets of pasta
1/2 kilo of cheese	3 cartons of milk
1 bag of rice	1 kilo of carrot

B Underline the correct alternatives.

A: Hi, Jo. Where are you?

B: Hi. I'm at the supermarket. I left the shopping list at work. Can I check some things? [1]*How much/ How many* fruit have we got?

A: Let me look. [2]*No/None.*

B: OK. [3]*How much/How many* vegetables [4]*is/are* there?

A: Lots, but we haven't got [5]*some/any* potatoes. And we need [6]*a/some* spaghetti. Maybe two packets?

B: Right. [7]*Is/Are* there [8]*a/any* water?

A: Yes, we've got [9]*a/some* bottle in the fridge, but we haven't got [10]*some/any* milk. Can you buy three cartons?

B: Sure. That's all, thanks. See you soon!

VOCABULARY   PREPOSITIONS

5 A Look at the picture and tick four true sentences. Correct the false sentences.

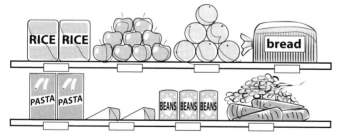

1 The oranges are next to the bread.
2 The cheese is between the beans and the carrots.
3 The pasta is behind the rice.
4 The apples are on the left of the oranges.
5 The grapes are in front of the carrots.
6 The bread is above the grapes and carrots.
7 The apples are between the rice and the oranges.
8 The beans are on the right of the carrots.

_____

_____

_____

_____

B ▶ R2.1 Listen and check.

VOCABULARY   LIFE STORY COLLOCATIONS

6 Write the verbs to complete the the sentences. All the verbs are in the past simple.

1 My grandfather w<u>ork</u>ed as a taxi driver when he was younger.
2 Kevin and Lisa g_____t married in 2013.
3 Vicki w_____t to school in London.
4 Diego Alvaro b_____e an actor when he was twenty-two.
5 When Ian was in his fourth year at university, he m_____t his future wife, Anna.
6 I w_____d for Samsung for three years – it was a good job.
7 After leaving university, Georgia g_____t a job as a personal assistant.
8 Nick was only twenty-eight when he s_____d his own company.

FUNCTION   SHOPPING; ORDERING IN A RESTAURANT

7 A Put the words in the correct order.

1 At a clothes shop

a) only / got / it / sorry, / we've / medium / in
   *Sorry, we've only got it in medium*_____.

b) help / can / you / I
   _____?

c) small / too / no, / it's
   _____.

d) large / in / got / this / you / have
   _____?

2 At a restaurant

a) yes, / like / with / potatoes / rice / I'd / chicken / and / the
   _____
   _____.

b) would / something / like / drink / and / you / to
   _____
   _____?

c) order / to / ready / you / are
   _____
   _____?

d) I / can / glass / of / water, / have / please / a / mineral
   _____
   _____?

B Put the conversations in Exercise 7A in the correct order.

1 At a clothes shop: _b_   _____   _____   _____
2 At a restaurant: _____   _____   _____   _____

CHECK

Circle the correct option to complete the sentences.

1 _____ a balcony?
a) Has it   **b)** Is there   **c)** Are there

2 Yesterday we _____ in the Czech Republic.
a) went   **b)** was   **c)** were

3 You can watch plays at the _____.
a) theatre   **b)** sports centre   **c)** cinema

4 We've got _____ butter in the fridge.
a) some   **b)** a   **c)** any

5 I _____ at home on Saturday.
a) staid   **b)** staied   **c)** stayed

6 Jessie and Karl got married _____.
a) two weeks ago   **b)** in two weeks   **c)** last two weeks

7 **A:** Can I help you?
B: Thanks, I _____.
a) just look   **b)** 'm just looking   **c)** just looking

8 We saw James _____.
a) the last week   **b)** a year ago   **c)** ago two months

9 _____ buy batteries here?
a) Can we to   **b)** We can   **c)** Can we

10 These jeans are _____ for me.
a) too big   **b)** not enough big   **c)** too much big

11 _____ of beans have we got?
a) How much tin   **b)** How much tins
c) How many tins

12 Don't stand _____ the television – I can't see!
a) behind   **b)** in front of   **c)** next to

13 We met _____ 2014.
a) on   **b)** in   **c)** at

14 Where _____ at the weekend?
a) you did go   **b)** did you go   **c)** did you went

15 Greg, _____ bread?
a) are there any   **b)** is there a   **c)** is there any

16 How much _____ have we got?
a) biscuits   **b)** toothpaste   **c)** bananas

17 The letter *D* is _____ *B* in the alphabet.
a) near   **b)** above   **c)** next to

18 _____ at the party last night?
a) Was Victor   **b)** Were Victor   **c)** Victor was

19 **A:** Are you ready to order?
B: Yes. _____ some chicken soup, please.
a) Could I   **b)** I like   **c)** I'd like

20 We had a great holiday. I _____ to come home.
a) no wanted   **b)** didn't wanted   **c)** didn't want

21 _____ you like any vegetables with your steak?
a) Would   **b)** Do   **c)** Are

22 **A:** Did you like the film?
B: Yes, _____.
a) I did like   **b)** I did   **c)** I liked

23 _____ visit the museum in the evenings?
a) Can you   **b)** You can   **c)** Do you can

24 Two _____ of coffee, please.
a) mugs   **b)** rolls   **c)** tubes

25 There _____ cheese on the table.
a) 's a   **b)** are some   **c)** 's some

26 I loved languages when I was at school, _____ I became an English teacher.
a) so   **b)** because   **c)** then

27 How _____ do we need?
a) many fruit   **b)** many eggs   **c)** much apples

28 Kieron, can you stand _____ Stefan, please?
a) on the right of   **b)** on left of   **c)** on the left

29 Do you like _____?
a) grape   **b)** grapes   **c)** a grape

30 **A:** That jacket looks good on you.
B: Thanks. _____
a) I have it.   **b)** I'll take it.   **c)** I'm not sure about.

RESULT   /30

VOCABULARY
TRAVEL ADJECTIVES

1 A Rewrite the sentences using the words in the box. There are two extra words.

> ~~empty~~ noisy cheap boring uncomfortable slow expensive quiet fast comfortable crowded interesting

1 There were no visitors in the museum.
The museum was _ empty _.

2 This bed's very hard – I can't relax on it.
This bed's _____.

3 The train travels at 165 kilometres an hour.
The train is very _____.

4 There were a lot of people on the beach.
The beach was _____.

5 The book's good and has a lot of useful information.
The book's _____.

6 The hotel is perfect – no cars outside, no children around, so I can sleep all day.
The hotel is _____.

7 The car was $35,000, so he didn't buy it.
The car was too _____ for him.

8 I didn't like the film. I slept for most of it.
The film was _____.

9 These jeans didn't cost a lot.
These jeans were quite _____.

10 I can't sleep because of the party in the flat below.
The party is very _____.

B ▶ **7.1** Listen and repeat the adjectives from Exercise 1A.

C Listen again and write the adjectives in the correct column for each stress pattern.

1 O	2 Oo
cheap	*empty*
3 Ooo	**4 oOo**
5 oOoo	

GRAMMAR
COMPARATIVES

2 Find and correct the mistakes in the sentences.

1 Hondas are popular than Suzukis.
Hondas are more popular than Suzukis.

2 South Africa's hoter than Italy.
_____

3 I'm more old than my brother.
_____

4 Indian food is spicyer than English food.
_____

5 Lena's intelligenter than me.
_____

6 Cola is sweetter than lemonade.
_____

7 Chinese is more difficult that English.
_____

8 Crisps are badder for you than chips.
_____

3 Complete the article with the comparative form of the adjectives in brackets.

EITHER ... OR ...?

We ask singer and actress Sonia Haig to choose. Which is better?

Q: Singing or acting?
A: Singing. Singing is [1]_____easier_____ (easy) for me than acting.

Q: Healthy food or junk food?
A: Junk food. I know healthy food is [2]_____ (good) for me, but after a concert, all I want is a pizza or a hamburger and chocolate!

Q: Relaxing on a beach or visiting an art gallery?
A: Oh, visiting an art gallery because it's [3]_____ (interesting). Sitting on a beach is boring.

Q: Dinner at a restaurant or dinner at home?
A: That's a difficult question. I like cooking, but I like having dinner at a restaurant because it's [4]_____ (romantic) than eating at home.

Q: Family or friends?
A: Family. I'm [5]_____ (close) to my sister than to my friends and I phone my parents every day.

Q: Summer or winter?
A: Well, I love looking at snow, but winter is [6]_____ (cold) and I prefer being hot. OK, summer.

Q: New York or Paris?
A: I love Paris, but I love New York more because it's [7]_____ (big) than Paris and I like all the shops. I have an apartment near Central Park.

Q: Cats or dogs?
A: Dogs. They're [8]_____ (friendly) than cats!

READING

4 A Read the emails. Are Tim and Mike good travel partners?

Hi Dan,

Mike and I arrived in Barcelona on Saturday. The first night we were in a self-catering apartment near the beach. I didn't sleep well because it was too noisy, so yesterday I moved to a hotel in the city centre. Mike stayed at the apartment because it's quite cheap. My hotel's very comfortable and quiet and it's got Spanish TV, so I can practise my Spanish in the evenings.

Yesterday Mike came with me to the Picasso Museum. I thought it was fantastic, but he wanted to leave after an hour. He said it was boring, so we went to the beach and met some local people and he talked to them for almost three hours – that was boring! Of course, he spoke in English because he doesn't know much Spanish.

Last night I wanted to go to a restaurant to try the local food, but Mike said it was too expensive. We went to a cheap snack bar and the food was awful.

Hope you're well.

Tim

Hi Lucy,

Tim and I are here in beautiful Barcelona. I'm in a self-catering apartment near the beach. It's not very comfortable, but I only go there to sleep. The first night there was a party next door and I danced until 3a.m. Tim said it was too noisy and he moved into a hotel in the city centre. He stays in his room in the evenings and watches TV! Can you believe it – watching TV on holiday?

Yesterday we went to the Picasso Museum. Well, it was OK for about an hour but Tim wanted to stay there all day! You know me – I like relaxing on the beach and meeting people. Yesterday I met some great people from Madrid and we chatted all afternoon.

Tim always wants to eat in expensive places, but I like buying food from shops and eating it on the beach. Last night we went to a snack bar. The food was terrible.

Mike

B Who says these things? Tim (T), Mike (M) or both (TM)?

1 I haven't got much money.   _M_

2 A good night's sleep is important for me.   _____

3 When I visit another country, I try to learn some of the language.   _____

4 We don't enjoy the same things.   _____

5 I love going to art galleries and museums.   _____

6 I talked to some Spanish people on the beach yesterday.   _____

7 I don't like eating expensive food.   _____

8 The food in the snack bar wasn't good.   _____

C Read the emails again and answer the questions.

1 Which is more expensive: the apartment or the hotel?
   _____the hotel_____

2 Which is further from the city centre: the apartment or the hotel?
   _____

3 Which is noisier in the evenings: the apartment or the hotel?
   _____

4 Which is more comfortable: the apartment or the hotel?
   _____

5 Who is more talkative: Tim or Mike?
   _____

6 Who is more serious: Tim or Mike?
   _____

7 Who is better at speaking Spanish: Tim or Mike?
   _____

8 Who is more laid back: Tim or Mike?
   _____

VOCABULARY

PLACES

1 Look at the pictures and complete the puzzle. Then find the hidden words: what do you have when you go on holiday?

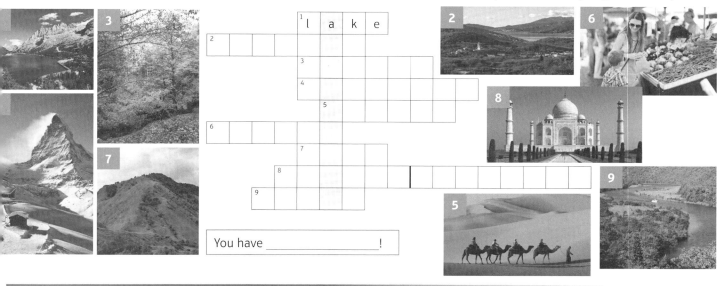

You have _____!

GRAMMAR

SUPERLATIVES

2 A Read the adverts. Which holiday is good for:
1 a family?
2 people who like relaxing?
3 people who like active holidays?

A   **Luxury weekend**

A relaxing weekend at the beautiful five-star Hanover Hotel. Swim in the warm sea and relax on the beach all day! Tennis courts and bicycles are available. The perfect laid-back holiday.

(3 nights – €1,490 per person)

B   **Mountain adventure**

Mountain biking in the Indian Himalayas – spend the day biking and sleep in tents at night. Prepare for temperatures of –10°C! A real adventure for the sporty holidaymaker.

(10 days – €2,490 per person)

C   **Family fun**

Camp Family has everything your children need to have a good time – a lovely blue lake, an adventure playground, mini-golf and go-karts. Stay in a self-catering apartment. Sit back, relax and let us give your children the holiday of a lifetime!

(6 days – €990 per family)

B Write sentences about the holidays using the superlative of the adjectives.
1 expensive *The most expensive is Mountain adventure.*
2 cheap _____
3 comfortable _____
4 noisy _____
5 long _____
6 easy _____
7 difficult _____
8 short _____
9 uncomfortable _____
10 cold _____

3 A Write questions using the prompts.
1 what / long / word in this sentence?
   What's the longest word in this sentence?
2 what / short / word on this page?
   _____
3 which / interesting / text in units 1–6 of this book?
   _____
4 which / good / exercise on this page?
   _____
5 what / difficult / grammar point in English?
   _____
6 who / happy / person in your family?
   _____
7 who / friendly / person in your English class?
   _____
8 which / bad / restaurant in your town?
   _____

B Answer the questions in Exercise 3A.

LISTENING

4 A ▶ 7.2 Look at the map and listen to Nick's audio diary. Does his train go to or from Moscow?

MOSCOW

SIBERIA

VLADIVOSTOK

B Read the sentences and check any new words in your dictionary.

1 The Trans-Siberian train journey takes nine days. _____F_____

2 The compartment is for two people. _____

3 Anton doesn't speak much English. _____

4 Nick can see snow, forests, villages, and lakes out of the window. _____

5 Nick and Anton buy food from women on the train. _____

6 They drink a lot of coffee on the train. _____

7 On the last evening of the journey, Nick went to a party. _____

8 Nick loved the Trans-Siberian train journey. _____

C Listen again. Are the sentences in Exercise 4A true (T) or false (F)?

D Correct the false sentences.

1 The Trans-Siberian train journey takes seven days.

_____

_____

_____

_____

_____

_____

_____

WRITING

CHECKING AND CORRECTING

5 A Read the extract from Nick's blog. Find and correct ten more mistakes with:

• spelling

• the past simple

• singular/plural forms.

Hi, it's Nick again. We started the day with a surprise – but not a good one. Anton and I ~~goed~~ *went* to the dining car for brekfast and there wasn't any food. That wasn't a big problem because I had some biscuit and we drinked some tea, but then we went back for lunch and it was the same situation. The waiter told us that there's a station where they usually get food, but the food truck wasn't there.

Nobody on the train was worried about this becaus almost everybody broght their own food. A guy called Egor gaves us half of his roast chicken and a Chinese couple gave us some bread. Peoples were so kind. Anton and I talked about how to thank them ... so I tought them some English songs and it were really just a big party. My best day on the train!

B Write about one day on a journey. It can be a real journey or an imaginary one. Write 80–100 words. Use Exercise 5A and these questions to help you.

• Where were you?

• How did you travel?

• What happened?

• Was it a good day?

C Check your work and correct any mistakes.

VOCABULARY
PLACES

1 Add the vowels to make places in towns.

1 sq*u* *a*r*e*
2 c_r p_rk
3 cr_ssr__ds
4 tr_ff_c l_ghts
5 c_rn_r
6 p_d_str__n str__t
7 p_rk
8 r__d

FUNCTION
GIVING DIRECTIONS

2 Look at the map of Dublin, Ireland, and complete the conversation. Speaker A is at Pearse Street station (START) and wants to go to the Tourist Information Office (TI).

A: Excuse me. Can you tell me the [1] ___*way*___ to the Tourist Information Office, please?

B: Sure. Go straight [2] _____ here, then turn [3] _____ into Lincoln Place and then right again into Nassau Street.

A: OK.

B: Then go [4] _____ on and go [5] _____ Kildare Street and Dawson Street.

A: OK, so I stay on Nassau Street.

B: Yes. [6] _____ past Grafton Street, into a small street … I forget the name … and the Tourist Information Office is on the [7] _____. You can't [8] _____ it.

A: Great. Thank you!

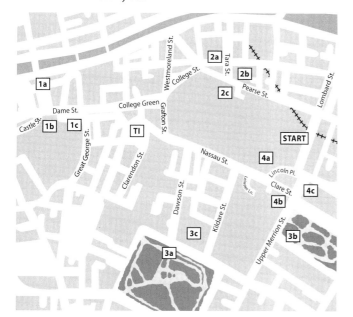

3 Read the information and look at the map in Exercise 2. Circle the correct alternatives.

Walking tours of Dublin

1 To Dublin Castle
From the Tourist Information Office, go to College Green and turn left. Go straight on to Dame Street, and turn left – that's Castle Street. It's on the left and number *1a/(1b)/1c* on your map.

2 From Dublin Castle to Trinity College
Go back to Dame Street and straight on to College Green and then turn left at College Street. Turn right, go straight on at Pearse Street, and then turn right again. It's number *2a/2b/2c* on your map.

3 From Trinity College to St Stephen's Green
Go back to Pearse Street and turn left, then left into College Street and then Grafton Street, and finally Nassau Street. Turn right into Dawson Street, and go straight on until the end. You can see it in front of you. It's number *3a/3b/3c* on your map.

4 From St Stephen's Green to the National Gallery
Come out of St Stephen's Green and look for Kildare Street. Go straight on and at the end of Kildare Street, turn right, and go straight on – that's Clare Street. The National Gallery is on your right, number *4a/4b/4c* on your map.

LEARN TO
CHECK AND CORRECT DIRECTIONS

4 A Look at the map and correct A's directions.

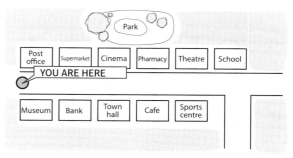

1 A: So, the park's between the cinema and the pharmacy.
B: No, it's _____*behind*_____ the cinema and the pharmacy.

2 A: So the supermarket's between the cinema and the pharmacy.
B: No, it's between _____.

3 A: So, the cinema is the fourth building on the left.
B: No, it's _____.

4 A: So, the café is the fourth building on the left.
B: No, it's _____.

5 A: So, the post office is opposite the bank.
B: No, it's opposite _____.

6 A: So, the town hall is opposite the bank.
B: No, it's _____ the bank.

B Circle the stressed words in B's answers in Exercise 4A.

1 B: No, it's (behind) the cinema and the pharmacy.

C ▶ 7.3 Listen and check. Then listen and repeat.

8 NOW

GRAMMAR
PRESENT CONTINUOUS

1 Write the *-ing* form of the verbs.

1 do _____*doing*_____
2 have _____
3 run _____
4 stay _____
5 swim _____
6 sleep _____
7 write _____
8 try _____
9 begin _____
10 give _____

2 A Complete the sentences with the present continuous form of the verbs in brackets.

1 Jake ___*'s singing*___ (sing).
2 Wesley _____ (take) a photo.
3 Jo and Dave _____ (stand) near Jake. They _____ (listen) to him.
4 Roger _____ (walk) near Jake, but he _____ (not listen) to him.
5 Megan _____ (sit) at the café. She _____ (read).
6 Paolo and Zoe _____ (chat) with each other. They _____ (not watch) Jake.
7 Lisa _____ (look) at some bags.
8 Philip _____ (sell) a bag to Kalila.

B Look at the picture and read the sentences in Exercise 2A again. Label the people in the picture.

C Write questions using the prompts.

1 what / instrument / Jake / play?
   What instrument is Jake playing?
2 who / Zoe / talk to?
   _____
3 where / Zoe and Paolo / sit?
   _____
4 how many bags / Jo and Dave / carry?
   _____
5 who / Wesley / take / a photo of?
   _____
6 who / talk / on the phone?
   _____
7 what / Megan / read?
   _____
8 who / buy / bag?
   _____

D Look at the picture and answer the questions in Exercise 2C.

1 *He's playing the guitar.*
2 _____
3 _____
4 _____
5 _____
6 _____
7 _____
8 _____

3 Put the words in the correct order to make questions. Then write short answers about you.

1 you / are / shoes / wearing
   Are you wearing shoes ? _Yes, I am./No, I'm not._

2 your / is / ringing / phone
   _____ ? _____

3 are / pen / a / with / exercise / this / doing / you
   _____ ? _____

4 room / other / the / sitting / are / people / in / any
   _____ ? _____

5 music / is / room / the / in / playing
   _____ ? _____

6 exercise / enjoying / are / this / you
   _____ ? _____

7 teacher / is / your / writing / the / board / on
   _____ ? _____

8 your / drinking / classmates / coffee / are
   _____ ? _____

VOCABULARY

VERBS + PREPOSITIONS

4 Complete the sentences with prepositions.

1 Dave's over there. He's chatting _with_ Joan.
2 I'm waiting _____ the train.
3 Diana, can you take a photo _____ the class?
4 What are you listening _____?
5 We read _____ the wedding yesterday in the newspaper.
6 I can't come at the moment. I'm talking _____ the phone.
7 Ask your teacher _____ the pronunciation of this word. I can't help you, sorry.
8 When I'm on holiday, I never think _____ work.

LISTENING

5 A ▶ 8.1 Listen and match conversations 1–5 with places a)–e).

Conversation 1 ⌐ a) tennis match
Conversation 2 ⌐ b) fashion show
Conversation 3 ⌐ c) art gallery
Conversation 4   d) concert
Conversation 5   e) ticket office

B Listen again and underline the correct alternative for each conversation.

1 The man _really likes_/doesn't like the paintings.
2 Nellie _wants_/ doesn't want to go to the concert.
3 The woman is _in_/going into a concert.
4 Felicity says she _wants_/doesn't want to meet for a coffee.
5 _All_/Some of the people are wearing black.

WRITING

PRONOUNS

6 A Read the story. Who took Julia's phone?

On Friday night, David, Julia and I went to the Rock Club. [1]Julia and David are fun and I like [2]Julia and David a lot. The club was busy, but [3]David, Julia and I found a table.

Julia put her mobile phone on the table, but after an hour [4]Julia saw that [5]Julia's phone wasn't there, and she was very angry. Then I had a good idea. I phoned [6]Julia's number, and [7]Julia, David and I heard [8]Julia's phone ringing.

David started laughing, and then [9]David took Julia's phone out of [10]David's pocket and gave [11]Julia's phone back to [12]Julia. David thought this was funny, but Julia was very angry with [13]David, so she took [14]David's phone and threw [15]David's phone out of the window! Now [16]David and Julia aren't speaking to each other.

B Replace the underlined nouns in the story with pronouns.

1 _they_ _____
2 _____
3 _____
4 _____
5 _____
6 _____
7 _____
8 _____
9 _____
10 _____
11 _____
12 _____
13 _____
14 _____
15 _____
16 _____

VOCABULARY

APPEARANCE

1 A Look at the photos and read the sentences. Label the men in the photos.

1 Rob's got curly hair. He's tall and very slim.

2 Sam's got short, straight hair, a moustache and a beard. He isn't wearing glasses.

3 Tom hasn't got a beard. He's got dark hair and he's medium build.

4 Bruce is very slim. He hasn't got short hair, but he's got a beard.

5 Mike isn't very slim. He's got very short, dark hair and he's wearing glasses.

6 Will's got dark, curly hair. He's got a beard and a moustache, and he's a little overweight.

B Describe the women in the photos.

1 Meg*'s got long, straight blonde hair and she's medium build* .

2 Jay _____ .

3 Keira _____ .

4 Belinda _____ .

2 Look at the photos and complete the crossword.

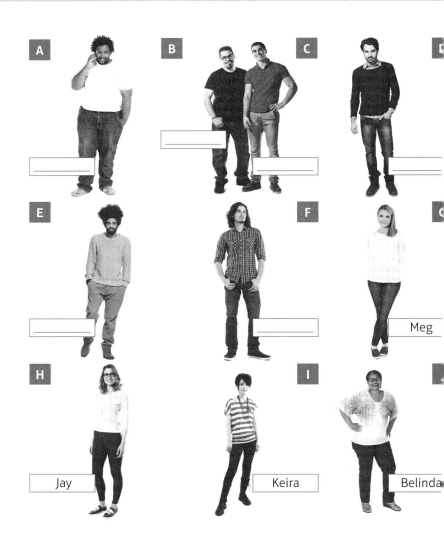

Across:

Down:

GRAMMAR
PRESENT SIMPLE AND CONTINUOUS

3 Underline the correct alternatives.

Gerald: Hi, Bruno. It's me, Gerald. What [1]*do you do/ are you doing?*

Bruno: I [2]*have/I'm having* a coffee with Carla. What about you?

Gerald: I [3]*sit/I'm sitting* at my desk as usual. So you [4]*don't work/aren't working* today.

Bruno: I am, but I [5]*don't usually start/I'm not usually starting* work before ten o'clock.

Gerald: How's Carla?

Bruno: OK, but she [6]*doesn't like/isn't liking* her job at the hospital.

Gerald: Oh, why not?

Bruno: Well, she [7]*works/'s working* from 11a.m. till midnight every day.

Gerald: That sounds hard. [8]*Does she look/Is she looking* for a new job?

Bruno: Yes, I think so. She [9]*looks/is looking* in the newspaper and on the internet every day.

Gerald: Really? Because [10]*I phone/I'm phoning* about a job opening here. Office work, not very interesting, but the money isn't bad. Perfect for Carla.

Bruno: Hey, Carla – good news, it's Gerald …

4 Complete the conversations with the present simple or present continuous form of the verbs in brackets.

Conversation 1

A: So who does the housework in your family?

B: We all [1]___*do*___ (do) it. In fact my wife [2]_____ (cook) dinner right now, and my daughter [3]_____ (help) her.

A: And what [4]_____ you _____ (do) to help at the moment?

B: I [5]_____ (watch) TV! There are too many people in the kitchen.

Conversation 2

A: Why [6]_____ (wear) black today? You [7]_____ (usually/not wear) black.

B: What do you mean? I always [8]_____ (wear) it!

Conversation 3

A: Hi, Geoff. It's me. Where are you?

B: I [9]_____ (stand) on the train.

A: Why? You [10]_____ (usually/not stand).

B: No, I usually [11]_____ (get) a seat, but this is a later train. Where are you?

A: I [12]_____ (wait) at the station.

B: Oh, sorry. I forgot to tell you I'm late!

READING

5 A Read the article. Are the sentences true (T) or false (F)?

1 T-shirts are 200 years old. ___F___

2 American soldiers were the first to wear T-shirts. _____

3 The most expensive T-shirts cost hundreds of pounds. _____

4 There are four different types of T-shirt. _____

5 T-shirts are popular because they are cheap. _____

6 You can change the message on an electronic T-shirt. _____

THE CHANGING T-SHIRT

It's an item of clothing many of us wear every day and it's often the only thing we wear on the top half of our body. After its introduction over 100 years ago as underwear for American soldiers, the T-shirt is now one of the most common items of clothing.

You can find T-shirts in any clothes shop and they cost between a few pounds to a few hundred pounds. There are even 'special' T-shirts that sell for thousands and thousands of pounds. And there are lots of different kinds of T-shirts: V-necks, U-necks, short-sleeved, long-sleeved, cropped T-shirts — you name it!

T-shirts are popular because they are more than just clothes: people can express themselves wearing T-shirts. A slogan on the front of your T-shirt can show people what you believe in; a T-shirt with your favourite band's logo can show people what kind of music you like; you can even wear your favourite photos by printing them on a T-shirt.

And the latest step in the development of the most popular item of clothing in the world? Electronic T-shirts. They light up when you wear them and they can even carry electronic messages that change when you programme them. What's next? Texting friends through T-shirts? It might be common very soon!

B Match words from the article 1–6 with definitions a)–f).

1 underwear
2 common
3 express
4 slogan
5 logo
6 programme

a) show your feelings, ideas or personality

b) give instructions to a computer, machine, etc.

c) a short, clever phrase that is easy to remember

d) clothes that you wear under your other clothes

e) a symbol for a group, organisation, etc.

f) happening often; that you see, hear, etc. very often

VOCABULARY
TYPES OF FILM

1 A Add the vowels to complete the types of film.

1 act_i_o_n f_i_lm
2 h_rr_r f_lm
3 sc_-f_ f_lm
4 m_s_c_l
5 r_m_nt_c f_lm
6 c_m_dy
7 dr_m_

B Match the extracts from film reviews with the types of film in Exercise 1A.

A

Ninety minutes in the scary world of vampires and blood ...   _2_

B

Childhood friends Jessica and Tim meet after ten years, and they want to be more than just good friends ... _____

C

Gene Walker is a modern-day Fred Astaire, dancing and singing his way through the streets of Cordoba ... _____

D

New York police officer Jack Hare takes a holiday in Miami, but finds himself working to save the country from a terrorist attack ... _____

E

A farmer in France wakes up and finds that all his animals can speak ... Chinese. Lots of laughs as the farmer teaches himself Chinese to talk to the animals. _____

F

A small Indian village has a visit from space tourists – aliens from another galaxy. A surprise as the aliens have more to learn from the locals than they think ... _____

G

Sally Bonner loses her parents in a train accident. She is blind and grows up alone with no friends ... but then Edmund, her teacher, helps Sally learn to play the piano. _____

FUNCTION
RECOMMENDING

2 Put the words in the box in the correct places in the conversation. You do not need two of the words.

| recommend   about (x2)   I   name   in   it   kind |

A: Do you want to watch a film?

B: Sorry, I'm busy.

                              recommend
A: Oh. Well then, ¹can you ⟨ a good film?

B: Hmm … ²What of films do you like?

A: Horror films, action films …

B: Do you like sci-fi?

A: I don't know many sci-fi films.

B: ³How *The Hunger Games*? Do you know it?

A: ⁴What's it?

B: It's about the future and the way rich people control us .

A: ⁵Who's it?

B: Jennifer Lawrence and Josh Hutcherson.

A: Oh, she's good.

B: Yeah. It's a good film – ⁶I think you'd like.

LEARN TO
LINK WORDS TO SPEAK FASTER

3 A ▶ **8.2** Listen and draw lines to show the linking.

1 Are you looking for‿a film?
2 Is it an action film?
3 Is anyone famous in it?
4 Do you want to watch a film?
5 I haven't got a DVD player.
6 I've got it on my computer.

B Listen again and repeat.

4 A ▶ **8.3** Listen and circle the sentence you hear.

1 a) Are you looking for a film?
   b) Are you looking for a friend?
2 a) Is it an action film?
   b) Is it an interesting film?
3 a) Is Anna Faris in it?
   b) Is anyone famous in it?
4 a) Do you want to borrow a DVD?
   b) Do you want to buy a DVD?
5 a) I haven't got a CD player.
   b) I haven't got a DVD player.

B Listen again and repeat.

VOCABULARY
ADJECTIVES

1 A Complete the article. Put the letters in order and write the words.

HOW DO YOU TRAVEL AROUND THE CITY?

I go to work by rollerblades. It's a ¹fast (asft) way to travel and it's very ²h_____ (ehtlhya) because I get lots of exercise. Sometimes it feels quite ³d_____ (dnesaurog) with so many cars around me, and it's a little ⁴i_____ (icnietnveonn) because I need to change into shoes when I go into my office. But rollerblades are a lot of fun.

Tony Jones, film producer

rollerblades

I go everywhere by skateboard. True, it takes a long time to learn because it's ⁵d_____ (idticulff) to ride one, but it's very ⁶c_____ (oeneintenv) – when I go into a shop, I just pick up the skateboard and carry it like a book!

Joel Williams, musician

skateboard

I use my scooter all around the city. It's ⁷s_____, (eafs) it's ⁸e_____ (yeas) to ride and it's more ⁹c_____ (forebltaome) than rollerblades or a skateboard because balancing isn't a problem. Sometimes you see scooters with motors on them, but those are really ¹⁰p_____ (tuinpogll). 'Go green,' I say!

Nanci Levine, student

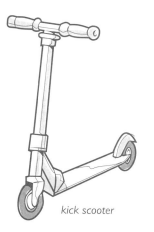

kick scooter

B ▶ 9.1 Listen and check.

C Listen again and write the adjectives in the correct column for each stress pattern. Then listen and repeat.

1 O	2 Oo
fast	
3 Ooo	4 oOo
5 oOoo	6 ooOoo

READING

2 A Read the article. How does the writer feel? Choose from the words in the box.

happy   relaxed   angry   hungry   funny

NO MORE WHEELS!
A shopkeeper speaks out

'I have a small food shop in the city centre and I really don't like customers coming into the shop on wheels. A businessman comes in on a kick scooter and he thinks it's funny to do his shopping *on* the scooter. I don't think it's funny – I think it's dangerous. And the skateboarders, they're even worse. They say they ride skateboards because it's fast and convenient – you know, it's easy to pick up the skateboard when they walk into a shop, but they don't pick up the skateboard, they ride it up and down my shop! But the worst of all are the rollerbladers. They fly into the shop; of course, they don't take off the rollerblades because it's inconvenient and they crash into customers and knock things down. It's terrible! So now I have a new rule: No more wheels. Shoes only!'

B Read the article again. Are the sentences true (T) or false (F)?

1 The writer has a restaurant.   *F*
2 He thinks the businessman is a funny person. _____
3 To the writer, kick scooters are not safe. _____
4 He thinks kick scooters are better than skateboards. _____
5 Skateboarders usually pick up their skateboards when they're in his shop. _____
6 Rollerbladers are the most dangerous, he thinks. _____

GRAMMAR

CAN/CAN'T, HAVE TO/DON'T HAVE TO

3 A Complete the conversations with the correct form of *can*.

1 A: _Can I park_ (I / park) my car here?
   B: No, _____. (you)
2 A: _____ (you / not ride) your bike on the pavement because it's too dangerous.
   B: Oh. OK.
3 A: _____ (people / smoke) on the train?
   B: No, _____ (they).
4 A: _____ (we / walk) to the theatre?
   B: Yes, _____ (we), but it's a long way.
5 A: _____ (taxis / drive) into the city centre, but not cars.
   B: OK, thanks.

B Complete the conversations with *can't* or *don't have to*.

Conversation 1

A: What clothes do you have to wear for the new job?
B: I _don't have to_ wear a suit and tie, but I have to wear a white shirt and I _____ wear jeans.

Conversation 2

A: It's late … after midnight.
B: Yes, but we _____ get up early tomorrow. It's Saturday.

Conversation 3

A: You _____ drive down this road. It's for buses only.
B: Oh, sorry.

Conversation 4

A: I haven't got any money with me.
B: It's OK. You _____ pay me now. Give me the money tomorrow.

4 Underline the correct alternatives.

A: Hey, do you want to do something tonight? I ¹*can't/don't have to* work.
B: Let's see … No, I ²*can't/don't have to* meet you tonight – I ³*can/have to* work late.
A: Well, ⁴*can we/do we have to* meet tomorrow?
B: Sorry, I ⁵*can't/don't have to*, I'm busy. But I ⁶*can/have to* do something on Saturday.
A: Great. We ⁷*can/have to* go to that new Italian restaurant, La Spezia.
B: Hmm … Saturday night is usually crowded. ⁸*Can we/Do we have to* book a table or ⁹*can we/do we have to* just go there?
A: It isn't so popular now, so we ¹⁰*can't/ don't have to* book. And if we ¹¹*can't/don't have to* get a table, we ¹²*can/have to* go somewhere else.
B: Great! See you on Saturday, then.

LISTENING

5 A Look at the picture of Carin Van Buren on her balancing scooter. Do you think the statements are true (T) or false (F)?

1 It's difficult to ride. _____
2 You can ride it on the pavement. _____
3 In a city it's faster than a bus. _____
4 It's tiring to ride. _____

B ▶ 9.2 Listen and check.

C Listen again and answer the questions.

1 Does Carin ride the scooter to work?
   Yes, she does.
2 How did she travel to work before?
   _____
3 How long does it take to learn?
   _____
4 How fast can the scooter go?
   _____
5 Does she think a scooter is better than a bike?
   _____
6 Where does she leave her scooter at work?
   _____
7 How does she feel when people laugh at her on her scooter?
   _____
8 Does she like it when people stop her and ask her questions?
   _____

VOCABULARY

TRANSPORT COLLOCATIONS

1 A Label the pictures.

bus

B Match sentences 1–9 with pictures A–I in Exercise 1A.

1 It's got two wheels, you get on and off it and it doesn't use petrol. ___C___

2 It's usually got two pilots and can carry a lot of people. _____

3 It's got four wheels and you pay the driver at the end of the journey. _____

4 It's got four legs and you ride it. _____

5 It's got two wheels and it uses petrol. _____

6 It's got hundreds of seats, but it can't go on a road. You need a ticket. _____

7 It moves on water. It can carry a lot of cars and people. _____

8 It moves on water. It can't carry a lot of people. _____

9 It's got wheels and it stops often. You pay at the start of the journey. _____

2 Complete the conversations with the correct form of the verbs in the box.

get off   go by (x2)   go on   take   ride   come by   get on

1 A: Can you tell me the way to the Sports Centre?
 B: Yes, you take the number 195 bus and you ___get off___ at the third stop.

2 A: Did you drive here?
 B: No, I _____ bus.

3 A: Is this Kenji's first bike?
 B: Yes, and he _____ it everywhere.

4 A: What's the best way to get to the airport?
 B: You can go by bus or you can _____ a taxi.

5 A: How do you go to school?
 B: I usually _____ foot.

6 A: How does Stefanie go to work?
 B: She _____ car.

7 A: Where are you?
 B: I'm at Berlin airport and I _____ a plane to South Africa, so I can't talk.

8 A: How did you travel to Paris?
 B: I _____ train.

READING

3 A Read the article and circle the correct options.

1 A *commute* is
   a) a type of transport.
   b) the journey from home to work and back.
   c) a part of a car.
2 Jim Kendrick won $10,000 because
   a) he was the safest driver in Texas.
   b) he drove the most kilometres in one year.
   c) he travelled the furthest to work.

DO YOU THINK YOUR COMMUTE IS BAD? TRY 640 KILOMETRES A DAY!

Do you think gas* prices are too high? Well, be happy that you aren't Jim Kendrick of Texas in the USA.

5   Every weekday, Kendrick drives 320 kilometres from his home in San Antonio, Texas, to his job at AbleCargo in the port of Houston and

10 then 320 kilometres back again! He leaves work at 5a.m. and gets home and has dinner with his wife at 9p.m.

15   For his daily journey, Kendrick won the competition 'America's Longest Commute'. His three-and-a-half-hour commute was longer than all the other people in the competition, and is a

20 lot more than the average American commute of twenty-five minutes.

    'I was surprised to win,' said Kendrick, who won $10,000. 'I was sure that someone else had a longer commute. But it's great – $10,000 is just enough to buy gas for another year.'

25 Why does he do it? 'Well, my wife and I have a beautiful house in San Antonio and our lifestyle is important to us. The drive also gives me a lot of energy. Sometimes, when I drive my Ford Mustang down the highway, I feel like a professional racing car driver.

30   How much longer does he want to do this commute? 'Another five or ten years,' Kendrick said. 'I don't see any reason to stop. But gas prices are high, so maybe I need to look for a job nearer home.'

*gas (American English) = petrol (British English)

B Read the article again and match the sentence halves. Then read the sentences and write the line number from the article where you found the information.

1 Jim won the contest because
   f – line 18
2 He was surprised to win because
   _____
3 He was happy about the money because
   _____
4 He does the commute because
   _____
5 He feels good when he drives because
   _____
6 He's thinking about changing jobs because _____

a) he doesn't want to change his lifestyle.
b) he spends about $10,000 a year on gas.
c) he thought someone else drove further.
d) gas prices are so high.
e) he feels like a racing car driver.
f) ~~his commute was the longest.~~

GRAMMAR
ARTICLES: A/AN, THE, NO ARTICLE

4 Complete the text with *a/an*, *the* or – (no article).

Jim lives in ¹_____*a*_____ house near ²_____ San Antonio, Texas. He's got ³_____ job at AbleCargo in ⁴_____ Houston, Texas, in ⁵_____ USA. AbleCargo is ⁶_____ shipping company, and Jim's ⁷_____ engineer there. He drives seven hours every day, and gets ⁸_____ home at 8.30 and has ⁹_____ dinner at 9p.m. He likes ¹⁰_____ fast cars, and he drives ¹¹_____ Ford Mustang. Jim doesn't commute at ¹²_____ weekend.

5 Add *a/an* (x4) and *the* (x6) to the sentences. One sentence does not need any extra words.

1 Yes, ⋏ bus station is down this street on ⋏ left.   *the* ... *the*
2 Rajiv is actor in Mumbai.
3 I haven't got car, but I've got motorbike.
4 Town Hall opens at 9.30 in morning.
5 I love planes and flying. I always ask for window seat.
6 Keith often works at home in evening.
7 Is Manchester in UK?
8 I often go home by taxi at night.

VOCABULARY
EXCUSES

1 Complete the excuses.
1 I didn't he _a r_ my al_ _ _ cl_ _ _.
2 I lo_ _ my ke_ _.
3 My car br_ _ _ d_ _ _.
4 The traf_ _ _ _ was bad.
5 I got up late and m_ _ _ _ _ the bus.

FUNCTION
APOLOGISING

2 A Put the words in the correct order to complete the conversation.

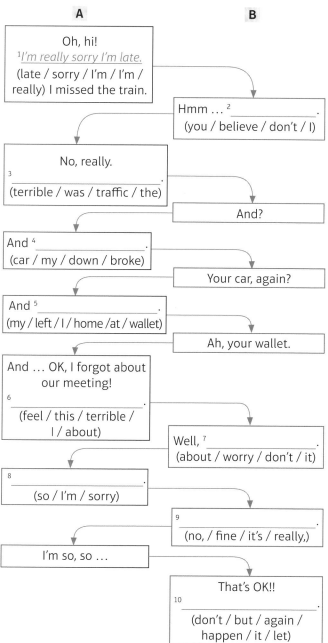

A

Oh, hi!
¹*I'm really sorry I'm late.*
(late / sorry / I'm / I'm / really) I missed the train.

No, really.
³_____.
(terrible / was / traffic / the)

And ⁴_____.
(car / my / down / broke)

And ⁵_____.
(my / left / I / home /at / wallet)

And ... OK, I forgot about our meeting!
⁶_____.
(feel / this / terrible / I / about)

⁸_____.
(so / I'm / sorry)

I'm so, so ...

B

Hmm ... ²_____.
(you / believe / don't / I)

And?

Your car, again?

Ah, your wallet.

Well, ⁷_____.
(about / worry / don't / it)

⁹_____.
(no, / fine / it's / really,)

That's OK!!
¹⁰_____.
(don't / but / again / happen / it / let)

B ▶ 9.3 Listen and check.

LEARN TO
TELL A LONG STORY

3 A Complete the story with the words in the box.

~~first of all~~   and   but   so   because (x2)   then   finally

We had a terrible day at the airport. ¹ _____*First of all*_____, we arrived forty minutes late ² _____ we missed our train. We were worried that we might miss the plane ³ _____ they don't let you get on when you're not there in time. ⁴ _____, when we got to the airport, we found that the plane wasn't on time, ⁵ _____ we went for a coffee at the airport café ⁶ _____ started talking to some people. They were very interesting and we had a nice chat. ⁷ _____, we got on the plane. When we found our seats, Jane looked for her bag, ⁸ _____ it wasn't there. It was at the café!

B Write Bruce's email using the prompts.

Dear Alexis,

I'm really sorry about last night. I know it was your birthday. But I had an unlucky evening …

First of all, I / leave / the house late because I / lose / my keys.

Then I / miss / the bus, so I / phone / a taxi, but the taxi / break down / and I / wait / thirty minutes for another taxi.

After that, I / get / to the restaurant an hour late, but I / leave / your present in the taxi.

I / phone / the taxi company, but they / not answer, so I / go / into the restaurant, but you / not be there.

Finally, I / go / home and / try / to phone you, but you / not answer.

Now I don't know what to do. I'm really sorry.

Love,

Bruce

First of all, I left the house late because…
_____
_____
_____
_____
_____
_____
_____
_____
_____
_____
_____
_____
_____
_____

GRAMMAR   VERB FORMS

1 A Underline the correct alternatives.

Jesse McCormack is a member of the rock group the Stringers. He ¹*writes/is writing* most of the band's songs and ²*plays/is playing* lead guitar. This is his summer festival blog.

Saturday 4th August

I ³*write/'m writing* my blog today at our fourth festival this summer ... but it's the biggest with more than 25,000 people and we ⁴*have/'re having* a great time. The atmosphere here is amazing and people are very friendly. We usually ⁵*arrive/are arriving* the day before we play, but this time we ⁶*come/came* here two days ago.

Most people have tents, but in fact you ⁷*don't have to/can't* sleep in a tent. You ⁸*can/can't* sleep in your car. And there are the usual festival rules, for example you ⁹*can/can't* use glasses for drinks – you ¹⁰*have to/don't have to* use plastic cups. This is a good idea because sometimes people, often children, ¹¹*walk/are walking* around with no shoes on.

There's only one hour before we start our show. Danny ¹²*talks/'s talking* to a woman from Radio One. Saul ¹³*practises/is practising* our first song. Our manager, Dave, ¹⁴*calls/is calling* us so I ¹⁵*have to/can* stop now. More tomorrow!

B Complete the interview with the correct present simple or present continuous form of the verbs in brackets.

Janna: This is Janna Towli from Radio One and I ¹*'m talking* (talk) to Danny Wright from the Stringers. Hi, Danny.

Danny: Hi, everyone.

Janna: So Danny, ²_____ (you / enjoy) yourself at the festival?

Danny: Yeah, it's cool.

Janna: We've got some questions. First, from Luka. He asks: '³_____ (Jesse / write) all the songs or ⁴_____ (you / write) any of them?'

Danny: Oh, Jesse is the songwriter. I just ⁵_____ (sing) the songs.

Janna: And from Viktoria: 'What's your favourite Stringers song?'

Danny: Erm … *You Never* ⁶_____ (say) '*I Love You.*'

Janna: OK, right. And the last question, from Abby. She asks: 'What ⁷_____ (Danny / wear) today?'

Danny: Me? Well, today I ⁸_____ (wear) a Stringers T-shirt and jeans. My usual! Oh, there's Dave, our manager. I have to go.

Janna: Thanks for talking to us. Good luck with the show!

Danny: Thanks!

VOCABULARY   ALPHABET PUZZLE

2 Complete the sentences with words beginning with the letters A–Z.

A I'm sorry I'm late. I didn't hear my ____*alarm*____ clock.

B My grandfather had a moustache and a big black ____*beard*____.

C The tram stop is close to my flat, so it's very _____ for me.

D Riding a bike is quite _____, so you have to wear a helmet.

E The opposite of *full* is_____.

F The White House is one of the most _____ buildings in the world.

G I want to see the Eiffel Tower. Where do I _____ off the bus?

H *Frankenstein* was one of the first _____ films. It was quite scary.

I The opposite of *boring* is _____.

J Fast food is sometimes called _____ food.

K Do you _____ the way to the bus station?

L The water in the _____ is very cold. We can't swim there.

M I got up late and I _____ my train.

N The children in the next room are too _____ – I can't work.

O Do you go by car or _____ foot?

P Cars are more _____ than bikes. Bikes are greener.

Q _____! The baby's sleeping.

R Can you _____ a good DVD?

S The map says that Via Lagrange is a pedestrian _____.

T I was late because the _____ was bad.

U Alan's shoes are too small, so they're very _____.

V She was born in a small _____ in Belgium.

W The traffic is _____ at five o'clock than at three o'clock.

X The opposite of *cheap* is e_____.

Y Hi, Liz. It's Jon. I waited for _____ for two hours! What happened?

Z My holiday was great. We saw the Great Wall. It was ama_____!

GRAMMAR COMPARATIVES AND SUPERLATIVES

3 Complete the text with the correct comparative or superlative form of the adjectives in the box.

| ~~good~~ tall cheap hot quiet interesting slow convenient cold fast |

SHANGHAI

When is the best time to go?

The ¹____best____ months to visit are May and October, when it's 19–24°C. July and August are ²_____ months, when it can be 28°C. November to April are ³_____ months, when it's 3–14°C.

How can I get around?

You can travel by bus or by metro. Buses are ⁴_____ than the metro, especially in the morning and evening when the traffic is bad. The metro is ⁵_____ than buses, but there are only two metro lines. The ⁶_____ way to travel around the city is by taxi because there are lots – they go everywhere and they aren't very expensive.

I only have one day! What can I see?

Visit ⁷_____ building in China, the 492-metre Shanghai World Financial Centre. The floor is glass and it feels like walking in the sky. Walk along the Bund, next to the river – it's very central, but it's a lot ⁸_____ than the noisy city centre. And visit the Shanghai Museum – most visitors to the city say this is ⁹_____ thing to see in Shanghai.

Where can I stay?

Shanghai has hundreds of hotels, and there are many two-star and three-star hotels for travellers on a budget – of course, these are ¹⁰_____ than the 4-star luxury hotels. Check the internet for recommendations from other travellers.

FUNCTION RECOMMENDING; GIVING DIRECTIONS

4 A ▶ R3.1 Listen to the conversations and circle the correct option.

Jurgen recommends a restaurant to Greg but
a) Greg doesn't understand and takes the wrong street.
b) he gives bad directions and Greg doesn't find the restaurant.
c) Greg decides to stay home and eat pizza.

B Listen again. Are the sentences true (T) or false (F)?

1 It's Jurgen's wife's birthday. _F_
2 Greg and his wife like Chinese food. _____
3 Jurgen recommends a Chinese restaurant. _____
4 The restaurant is near the cinema. _____
5 Greg and his wife find the restaurant. _____
6 They have pizza at the restaurant. _____

C Listen again and complete the sentences.

1 What kind of food _do you like_?
2 Do you think my wife _____?
3 Can you tell _____?
4 Go down Hillside Road past the pharmacy _____.
5 Then go straight _____ 200 metres.
6 Oh, no – I'm so _____.
7 I feel terrible _____.
8 Don't worry _____.

GRAMMAR ARTICLES

5 Complete the text with *a/an, the* or – (no article).

POLAND – DAY 7

The best way to see ¹_the_ city of ²_____ Krakow is in ³_____ Trabant – the classic eastern-European car. The tour starts at 9.00a.m. in ⁴_____ city centre, where you meet your tour guides Irek and Kasia. Irek is ⁵_____ university student and Kasia is ⁶_____ history teacher, and together they know Krakow better than most professional guides. You start the tour on ⁷_____ foot and visit Cloth Hall in ⁸_____ centre of Grand Square. You then go by ⁹_____ car and visit Nowa Huta and the Jewish quarter. Lunch is at ¹⁰_____ restaurant near the castle. ¹¹_____ Polish food is quite rich, so try not to eat too much! In ¹²_____ afternoon, Irek and Kasia can show you Wawel Castle or take you back to your hotel.

57

CHECK

Circle the correct option to complete the sentences.

1 Sitting on the beach is _____ working.
   a) relaxing than   **b)** better than
   c) more nice than

2 There was a bridge over the _____.
   a) desert   **b)** river   **c)** mountain

3 I _____ my MP3 player.
   a) listening to   **b)** 'm listenning to
   c) 'm listening to

4 What _____ like?
   a) does Jon look   **b)** Jon does look   **c)** Jon looks

5 **A:** Do I _____ the bus here for the museum?
   B: No, at the next stop.
   a) go by   **b)** ride   **c)** get off

6 I didn't get a seat because the train was _____.
   a) comfortable   **b)** uncomfortable   **c)** crowded

7 Sorry I'm late. I _____ my train.
   a) lost   **b)** missed   **c)** left

8 **A:** What _____?
   B: I'm working on the computer.
   a) you are doing   **b)** are you doing
   c) do you doing

9 I don't think _____ this DVD. It's too scary.
   a) you'd like   **b)** you like   **c)** you recommend

10 My wife works _____. She's a writer.
   a) at home   **b)** at the home   **c)** home

11 _____ to the airport by bus?
   a) You can go   **b)** Do you can go   **c)** Can you go

12 Go _____ until the end of the street.
   a) straight   **b)** straight on   **c)** strait on

13 It was difficult to walk in the _____ because of all the trees.
   a) mountain   **b)** forest   **c)** village

14 The children _____ very well at the moment.
   a) aren't feeling   **b)** don't feeling   **c)** aren't feel

15 He _____ slim with short black hair.
   a) 's got   **b)** 's   **c)** has

16 Spanish is _____ than English.
   a) easyer   **b)** easier   **c)** more easy

17 Children _____ pay. It's free for them.
   a) don't have to   **b)** can't   **c)** haven't to

18 **A:** I laughed a lot at this DVD. It's very funny.
   B: Oh, so it's a _____.
   a) drama   **b)** musical   **c)** comedy

19 **A:** Is there a post office near here?
   B: Yes, go down here and it's _____.
   a) on the left   **b)** on left   **c)** the left

20 I always go by underground because it's fast and _____.
   a) convenient   **b)** polluting   **c)** dangerous

21 It's _____ hotel in Saudi Arabia.
   a) the bigger   **b)** the bigest   **c)** the biggest

22 The sign says 'No Parking', so you _____ park here.
   a) have to   **b)** don't have to   **c)** can't

23 My grandmother is _____.
   a) in sixties   **b)** in her sixties   **c)** in the sixties

24 **A:** Do you often phone your parents?
   B: Yes, I talked to _____ last night.
   a) them   **b)** him and her   **c)** they

25 _____ is good for you.
   a) Milk   **b)** The milk   **c)** A milk

26 Who is _____ player in the football team?
   a) most bad   **b)** the worst   **c)** the baddest

27 _____, the train arrived. It was four hours late.
   a) First of all   **b)** After   **c)** Finally

28 Leonie _____ black.
   a) always is wearing   **b)** is wearing always
   c) always wears

29 **A:** Where's the tourist information centre?
   B: You _____ left and walk for about five minutes.
   a) take   **b)** turn to   **c)** turn

30 **A:** Have you got _____?
   B: No, I haven't, but I've got two brothers.
   a) a sister   **b)** the sister   **c)** sister

RESULT	/30

GRAMMAR

BE GOING TO; WOULD LIKE TO

1 A Look at the table and complete the sentences with the correct form of *be going to* or *would like to*.

	Plans for next week	Plans for next year	Wishes for the future
Jim, USA	start new job at the bank – Monday	look for a new flat not stay at parents' house	be very rich
Hiro, Japan	have haircut – Tuesday	go to university	work in TV
Tom and Kim, Ireland	visit daughter Lynn and family – Saturday/Sunday	not have a holiday	move nearer Lynn

Jim   Hiro   Tom and Kim

1 Jim *'s going to start* his new job at the bank on Monday.
2 He _____ for a new flat next year.
3 He _____ at his parents' house.
4 He _____ very rich.
5 Hiro _____ a haircut on Tuesday.
6 She _____ to university next year.
7 She _____ in TV.
8 Tom and Kim _____ their daughter at the weekend.
9 They _____ a holiday next year.
10 They _____ nearer their daughter.

B Write questions about the people in Exercise 1A using the prompts. Use *be going to* or *would like to*.

1 which bank / you / work at, Jim?
   Which bank are you going to work at, Jim?
2 where / you / look for / a new flat, Jim?
   _____
3 when / you / go / to university, Hiro?
   _____
4 why / like / work / in TV, Hiro?
   _____
5 how / you / travel, Tom and Kim?
   _____
6 why / like / move / nearer your daughter, Tom and Kim?
   _____

C Match answers a)–f) with questions 1–6 in Exercise 1B.

a) Because I want to be famous.   4

b) We're going to go by train.   _____
c) In the city centre.   _____
d) We'd like to see our grandchildren more.   _____
e) In September next year.   _____
f) At HACB bank.   _____

2 Put the words in the correct order to make questions. Then write short answers about you.

1 TV / you / to / evening / watch / are / this / going
   Are you going to watch TV this evening ?
   Yes, I am./No, I'm not.
2 like / work / would / TV / to / you / in
   _____ ?
3 weekend / you / family / see / next / are / to / going / your
   _____ ?
4 for / English / to / useful / be / you / is / going
   _____ ?
5 like / new / would / phone / a / you / buy / to / mobile
   _____ ?
6 your / study / classmates / year / you / going / English / next / to / are / and
   _____ ?
7 in / like / live / country / you / to / would / another
   _____ ?
8 home / your / like / now / to / go / would / classmates
   _____ ?

READING

3 A Read the article and circle the best title.

a) Lottery winners around the world
b) Jobless man wins lottery
c) Lottery winner starts organisation to help people

When Juan stopped to buy a lottery ticket last week, he didn't have a job or enough money to pay the bills. These were his last few coins. He picked seven numbers, and then asked another customer to pick the last number. 'I'll never win, anyway,' he thought. But he was wrong – he won £1.2 million!

First of all, he paid all his bills and then he went to buy two – yes, two – really, really expensive cars. But Juan isn't going to drive them – he never learnt to drive because he didn't have enough money to buy a car before. He bought them for his children, Carla and Paolo.

Winning the lottery isn't going to change Juan. He and his wife aren't going to spend their money without thinking. First, they are going to buy homes for their children and then they are going to have a long holiday in America. After that, Juan is going to start an organisation to help people without jobs because he was also unemployed and knows how hard it is.

B Read the article again and answer the questions.

1 How much money did Juan have when he bought the ticket?
A few coins.

2 Did he think he could win the lottery?
_____

3 How much money did he win?
_____

4 Who is going to drive the cars?
_____

5 Does he want to change his life?
_____

6 Who are Juan and his wife going to buy homes for?
_____

7 Who does Juan want to help with his organisation?
_____

VOCABULARY

PLANS

4 A Complete the puzzle with the words in the box and find the message.

| ~~time off~~ | married | stay | clubbing | learn |
| a holiday | start | move | some work | go for |

¹ t a k e **t i m e o f f**
² _ _ _ _ a w a l k
³ d o _ _ _
's
⁴ h a v e _ _ _
⁵ g o _ _ _
⁶ _ _ _ h o m e
⁷ g e t _ _ _
⁸ _ _ _ a n e w j o b
e
⁹ _ _ _ t o s w i m
¹⁰ _ _ _ i n _ _ _

Message: _____ !

B Complete the words in the conversations.

Conversation 1
A: What are you going to do this weekend?
B: I'm going ¹jo*gging*____ on Saturday morning and then in the evening I'm going to meet Bob and we're going for a ²dr_____ in the pub.

Conversation 2
A: So, what are your plans?
B: Well, we're going to get ³ma_____ next year and we'd like to ⁴mo_____ to another country – maybe Spain. We'd like to ⁵ge_____ a house there, and start a ⁶fa_____ – maybe have three or four children.

Conversation 3
A: What's your son going to do?
B: He's going to stay with some ⁷fr_____ in São Paulo. He wants to do a ⁸co_____ and ⁹le_____ Portuguese and then he'd like to get a ¹⁰jo_____ with a computer company in Brazil.

Conversation 4
A: What are you going to do with your lottery money?
B: First, I'm going to ¹¹ta_____ a break! I'm going to ¹²ha_____ a long holiday – and ¹³st_____ in a five-star hotel, of course!

Conversation 5
A: Are you going to have a ¹⁴pa_____ and invite all your friends?
B: Of course! And then I'm going to go ¹⁵sh_____ in Paris to buy some fantastic designer clothes.

VOCABULARY

PHRASES WITH GET

1 A Add the vowels to complete the phrases.

1 Marco got _sunburnt_ (snbrnt), so he
2 I got _____ (thrsty), so I
3 Adrian got _____ (trd) at school, so he
4 They got _____ (wt), so they
5 Ed and Leo got _____ (hngry), so they
6 I got very _____ (ht), so I
7 Helena got _____ (lst), so she
8 We got _____ (cld), so we
9 Ferdi got _____ (stng) by a bee, so he
10 Alice was cold, so to get _____ (wrm), she

B Match a)–j) with 1–10 in Exercise 1A to make sentences.

a) was an hour late for the meeting. _____
b) put some cream on his finger. _____
c) had a second breakfast. _____
d) went to sleep in the break. _____
e) changed into dry clothes. _____
f) had a hot bath. _____
g) went for a drink with Carson. _____
h) put on our coats. _____
i) stayed indoors for the next two days. ___1___
j) took off my sweater. _____

C ▶ 10.1 Listen and write the words in the correct column.

1 /ʌ/ e.g. cup	2 /ɒ/ e.g. job	3 /e/ e.g. red
	hot	
4 /ɜː/ e.g. her	5 /ɔː/ e.g. four	6 /əʊ/ e.g. go

2 Look at meanings 1–4 of *get* in the table. Then write the words below in the correct column.

1 become	2 arrive	3 buy	4 obtain
get … *hungry*	get …	get …	get …

to school   hungry   a new computer   some help

a present for a friend   to work   a new car   home

a glass of water   a job   lost   tired

LISTENING

3 A ▶ 10.2 Listen to four people who survived in difficult situations. Match speakers 1–4 with places a)–d).

Speaker 1   a) jungle
Speaker 2   b) mountain
Speaker 3   c) desert
Speaker 4   d) sea

B Listen again and circle the correct options.

1 Speaker 1 _____
 a) ate fish.
 b) drank seawater.
 c) was cold.

2 Speaker 1 _____
 a) got sunburnt.
 b) got tired.
 c) saw a lot of sharks.

3 Speaker 2 _____
 a) got cold.
 b) walked all day.
 c) got very thirsty.

4 Speaker 2 _____
 a) saw lots of insects.
 b) had food with her.
 c) sometimes took her shoes off.

5 Speaker 3 _____
 a) was on the mountain for three nights.
 b) got lost because of the snow.
 c) made a fire.

6 Speaker 3 _____
 a) slept on the ground.
 b) got hungry.
 c) stayed warm.

7 Speaker 4 _____
 a) got very hungry.
 b) got thirsty.
 c) didn't get bored.

8 Speaker 4 _____
 a) had some food with her.
 b) ate plants.
 c) ate insects.

GRAMMAR

WILL, MIGHT (NOT), WON'T

4 Complete the sentences with *will* or *won't* and the verbs in the box.

| get   be (x2)   miss   win   come   know   love |

1 Wear your coat or you *'ll get* _____ cold.
2 Do you think Brazil _____ the World Cup?
3 It's very late. I'm sure the shop _____ open.
4 I don't want to go to the party! I _____ any people there.
5 Come on! We _____ the train.
6 Read this book. I'm sure you _____ it.
7 Oh no! I'm late again. The boss _____ happy.
8 You can invite Alain, but he _____ . He doesn't like jazz music.

5 Underline the correct alternatives.

SURVIVE
IN THE CITY

People always talk about survival in the jungle, at sea, etc., but I'll tell you a really dangerous place: the city! Here are my tips for survival.

- Don't drive. Traffic is usually terrible and you ¹*might not/'ll/won't* spend more time in your car than seeing the city.

- Ask people for help – most people ²*will/might/won't* be happy to stop and help you.

- Don't stand in the street with a map in your hand and a camera around your neck. People ³*will/ might not/won't* know you're a tourist. That's not a problem, but someone ⁴*will/might/might not* come and take your money.

- Wear normal clothes, not expensive ones. With expensive clothes, people ⁵*will/might not/won't* think you've got lots of money and yes – they ⁶*'ll/ might/won't* take it away from you!

- Carry an umbrella. It often rains and with an umbrella you ⁷*'ll/might/won't* get wet.

- Don't stay out too late or it ⁸*'ll/might/might not* be easy to find a bus or a taxi.

- Give waiters a good tip, maybe 10%. You ⁹*'ll/might/might not* go back to the same restaurant and the waiter ¹⁰*will/might not/won't* forget you!

6 ▶ 10.3 Listen and number each pair of sentences in the order you hear them.

1 a) You'll get cold.   _2_
   b) You get cold.   _1_
2 a) We'll miss the train.   _____
   b) We miss the train.   _____
3 a) I'm sure you'll hate it.   _____
   b) I'm sure you hate it.   _____
4 a) They'll know you're a tourist.   _____
   b) They know you're a tourist.   _____
5 a) I'll stay at home.   _____
   b) I stay at home.   _____
6 a) I'll never go out.   _____
   b) I never go out.   _____

WRITING

TOO, ALSO, AS WELL

7 Are *too*, *also* and *as well* in the correct place? Tick three correct sentences. Correct the wrong sentences.

1 The bus is a good way to travel and the underground is too good. ✗
2 If you buy a travel card for the underground, you can also use it on the bus.
3 You can ask shopkeepers for help – they're very friendly and they'll know the city as well.
4 It's generally a safe city, but it can be dangerous also to walk alone late at night in some areas.
5 It isn't a good idea to carry a lot of money, and leave your expensive watch too at home.
6 You can get delicious food in cafés and as well in street markets.
7 Don't walk too far and also wear comfortable shoes – then you won't get tired.
8 At night, taxis are as well convenient, but they're expensive.

8 Write a short text giving advice for a visitor to your town or city. Use *too, also, as well* and these phrases to help you. Write 80–100 words.

The … is a good way to travel …

It's a good idea to carry …

You can ask … for help, and you can ask …

It can be dangerous to …

VOCABULARY
ART AND CULTURE

1 Put the letters in the correct order to make words connected with art and culture. Then write them in the correct place in the crossword.

ILFM	F _ILM_
INATPIGN	P _____
RWGIAND	D _____
AORPOGHHTP	P _____
TESAUT	S _____
EHIXTOINIB	E _____
EACND EPNAMRCEOFR	D _____
OCETNER	C _____
LPYA	P _____

[crossword grid with numbered cells 1–8, cell 5 filled in as F I L M]

FUNCTION
MAKING SUGGESTIONS

2 Complete the conversation with the words in the box. There are two extra words.

~~why~~	shall	how	don't	about	let's	have	stay

Tim: Gordon, ¹ _why_ don't we do something different this evening?

Gordon: I don't know. Have you got any ideas?

Tim: How ² _____ going to a concert?

Gordon: Hmmm … That might be difficult. We don't like the same music. You like rock, I like hip hop.

Tim: Oh. That's true. ³ _____ we invite some friends over?

Gordon: I don't really feel like doing that.

Tim: OK then. Why ⁴ _____ we ⁵ _____ home and watch TV?

Gordon: That's a good idea. What's on?

Tim: Let me see … Uh, *Prometheus* by Ridley Scott.

Gordon: Brilliant!

Tim: And ⁶ _____ have popcorn, too.

Gordon: Sounds good!

LEARN TO
RESPOND TO SUGGESTIONS

3 A Correct the mistakes in suggestions 1–5 and responses a)–e).

1 Let ᵗˢ go shopping. _e_

2 How about go for a bike ride? _____

3 Why don't we going to an art gallery? _____

4 What about staying at home and cook something? _____

5 Who about making spaghetti and meatballs? _____

a) It's not for. Looking at paintings is boring!

b) I don't really feel like do that. I'm too tired.

c) That a good idea. You make the meatballs, I can make the pasta.

d) Brilliant! What we shall eat?

e) That isn't very good idea. I haven't got much money.

B Match the suggestions with the responses in Exercise 3A.

11 HEALTH

VOCABULARY

THE BODY; HEALTH

1 A Find twelve words for parts of the body in the puzzle.

N	M	O	E	L	B	O	W
O	T	H	U	M	B	I	V
S	L	E	G	U	T	M	B
E	K	N	E	E	O	O	A
P	H	E	A	D	E	U	C
E	E	N	E	C	K	T	K
S	T	O	M	A	C	H	C
W	E	H	A	N	D	I	N

B ▶ 11.1 Listen and repeat.

C Listen again and write the words in the correct column.

1 /e/ e.g. *red*	2 /æ/ e.g. *happy*
3 /iː/ e.g. *meat*	**4 /əʊ/ e.g. *no***
	elbow
5 /ʌ/ e.g. *fun*	**6 /aʊ/ e.g. *now***

2 Put the letters in the correct order to make health problems. Start with the underlined letter.

1 I've got a ___cold___, so I must stay in bed today. (d<u>c</u>lo)
2 My leg _____. (<u>sh</u>utr)
3 I've got a bad _____. (<u>ch</u>adeeha)
4 I've got a _____ _____. (ro<u>s</u>e <u>t</u>rahot)
5 I've got a _____. (n<u>r</u>nuy os<u>n</u>e)
6 I've got an awful _____. (caha<u>st</u>cehom)
7 I've got a _____. (me<u>tt</u>erupare)
8 I've got a _____. (gu<u>c</u>oh)

GRAMMAR

SHOULD/SHOULDN'T

3 Read the leaflet about travel health. Check any new words in your dictionary. Then complete the leaflet with *should/shouldn't* and the words in brackets.

> ### TRAVEL HEALTH: BEFORE YOU GO
>
> We answer your FAQs (frequently asked questions) about health on holiday:
>
> [1] *Should I see* (I/see) my doctor before I go on holiday?
>
> Yes, [2] _____ (you/speak) to your doctor or your local travel centre about six weeks before you leave.
>
> [3] _____ (I/get) any vaccinations?
> Your doctor or nurse can give you information or you can check on the internet. [4] _____ (you/not have) a lot of vaccinations together, so start early.
>
> What else [5] _____ (I/do)?
> [6] _____ (you/visit) your dentist as well, because dentists can be very expensive in other countries.
> [7] _____ (you/take) a Traveller's First Aid Kit with sun cream, plasters and painkillers, but [8] _____ (you/not open) these before you travel. Officials at the airport might ask to check them.
>
> Any other advice?
> Well, [9] _____ (you/not travel) when you have a bad earache or a cold. And it's important to relax, but [10] _____ (you/not drink) alcohol or coffee in the airport or on the plane, because they'll make you feel worse.

4 Complete the conversation with *should/shouldn't* and the verbs in the box. Add the correct pronouns (*I* or *you*).

go (x2)   watch   sleep   do (x2)   change   eat

A: I'm going to fly to Japan soon and I'm worried about the time difference, you know, getting tired after the journey.
B: Oh yes, jet lag can be difficult. [1] *You should go* to bed early for two or three nights before you travel.
A: What else [2] _____?
B: When you're on the plane, [3] _____ all the food they bring, it's too much. And [4] _____ your watch to Japanese local time.
A: And [5] _____ on the plane?
B: Yes, you need to rest, so [6] _____ all the movies or stay awake the whole time. It's a long journey! What time do you arrive?
A: At two in the afternoon.
B: You'll be very tired, but [7] _____ to bed. [8] _____ some exercise. It's a good idea to go for a walk and then wait and sleep when it's dark.
A: Thanks. That's good advice.

Walking – the perfect sport?

Forget about tennis, swimming, skiing and jogging. Walking is the easiest and cheapest way to stay fit. It's free, you don't need special clothes or equipment, you don't need a trainer or a special place. Anybody can do it any time: young people, older people, alone or in groups.

OK – perhaps it's not really a sport, but it is the most popular physical activity and one of the best ways to stay healthy. What are the benefits? Walking is good for your heart and your legs; regular walkers say they sleep better and feel happier; and smokers say they don't smoke so much.

Maybe you don't have very much time, so here are some ideas to help you start walking:

- Walk, don't drive, to the local shop. If you have a lot to carry, take a small backpack.

- If you have children, walk with them to and from school.

- Get off the bus or train a stop or two early. This will give you some extra daily exercise – and it's cheaper, too!

- Take a walk in your lunch hour at school or work.

- Once a week take a longer walk, and go on a completely new route; this helps to keep things interesting.

There are walkers' clubs all over the world. Join one – walking is a great way to meet people and make new friends!

READING

5 **A** Read the article and number topics a)–d) in the order that you read about them.

a) Why is walking better than other sports?   *1*
b) How can you find time for walking?   ___
c) Who can you walk with?   ___
d) Why is walking good for your health?   ___

B Read the article again and tick the ideas it talks about.

1 Walking isn't expensive.   ✓
2 You have to wear good walking shoes.   ___
3 Age isn't important.   ___
4 Walking is good for headaches.   ___
5 You should go shopping on foot.   ___
6 Get up earlier in the morning, and do some extra exercise every day.   ___
7 Take a different walk every week so you don't get bored.   ___
8 You can meet people more easily when walking.   ___

C Find words 1–7 in the article. Then match them with definitions a)–g).

1 equipment
2 a trainer
3 alone
4 physical
5 benefits
6 a backpack
7 a route

a) with no other people
b) a bag that you carry on your back
c) connected to your body
d) the things you use for an activity, e.g. a machine in the gym
e) a way from one place to another
f) good things
g) a teacher

D Cover the article and try to complete the sentences. Then look at the article and check your answers.

Maybe you don't have very much time, so here are some ideas to help you start walking:

- Walk, don't drive, [1]_____ the local shop. If you [2]_____ a lot to carry, take a small backpack.

- If you [3]_____ children, walk [4]_____ them to and [5]_____ school.

- Get off the bus or train a stop or two early. This will give you some extra daily exercise – and it's cheaper, [6]_____!

- Take a walk [7]_____ your lunch hour [8]_____ school or work.

- Once a week [9]_____ a longer walk, and go on a completely new route; this helps to keep things interesting.

There are walkers' clubs [10]_____ over the world. Join one – walking is a great way to [11]_____ people and [12]_____ new friends!

VOCABULARY
COMMUNICATION

1 A Complete the diagrams with the verbs in the box.

start finish forget get send have answer (x2) turn on exchange remember turn off

1   _start_
    finish ⟩ a conversation
    _____

2   _____
    _____ ⟩ a text message
    _____

3   _____
    _____ ⟩ names and numbers
    _____

4   _____
    _____ ⟩ your phone
    _____

B Complete the sentences with the verbs in Exercise 1A.

1 Sorry, I have to go now. Can we ___finish___ the conversation now and talk again later?

2 I'll _____ you a text message when I get home.

3 I'm sorry, I don't _____ your name – I've got a terrible memory.

4 Please _____ your phone. The play is starting.

5 I can't _____ his text message now – I'm busy. I'll do it later.

6 Good to see you again! Let's _____ numbers so we can talk again soon.

7 The two of you need to _____ a conversation – you should talk about this.

8 Please _____ your phone – it's ringing, again! And tell your friend that you are in a meeting and can't talk right now!

9 I always _____ my mobile number. I have to write it down.

10 I didn't want to talk about this. I didn't _____ the conversation – you did.

11 The play's over – you can _____ your phone now.

12 When did you _____ this text message from Ewan? What does it say?

LISTENING

2 A ▶ 11.2 Listen to a radio programme about time management. Number the problems in the order you hear about them.

multi-tasking	_____	_____
forgetting things you have to do	_____	_____
staying late to finish work	_____	_____
doing what you like doing first	_____	_____
starting work without planning	_1_	_d_
keeping two or three lists of things to do	_____	_____

B Listen again and match the problems in Exercise 2A with solutions a)–f).

a) Write a to-do list.

b) Do one thing, then do another thing.

c) Don't try to finish something if you are tired.

d) Make time to plan your day and week.

e) Make only one list.

f) Put the important things at the top of your list.

C Complete the guide for the radio programme with the words in the box. There are two extra words.

professor multi-task same hour use time management improve make

Working Week

with Patti Fry
5.30p.m.–6.30p.m.

In today's Working Week, Patti Fry talks to [1]Professor Emma Fields and asks why some people [2]_____ their time better than others. She also asks how to [3]_____ our time at work by using different [4]_____ techniques. Emma gives us some useful ideas for working better. One of them is: don't [5]_____ – do one thing first, then another. Doing two or more things at the [6]_____ time isn't such a good idea.

GRAMMAR

ADVERBS OF MANNER

3 Underline the correct alternative.

1 A: Your mum drives really *slow/slowly*.

  B: Yes, well you know that *slow/slowly* drivers don't have many accidents.

2 A: Jeff is quite *lazy/lazily* about doing tasks around the house.

  B: That's true, he does them *lazy/lazily*, but he does them in the end!

3 A: The teacher talks very *quiet/quietly*.

  B: Yes, and the students aren't *quiet/quietly*, so it's difficult to hear.

4 A: I found the shop *easy/easily*, thanks to your clear directions.

  B: Well, in fact, it's rather *easy/easily* to find.

5 A: Our team played *bad/badly* and we lost the match.

  B: That's surprising, I thought the other team was *bad/badly*.

6 A: You're so *energetic/energetically* when you get up in the morning. How do you do it?

  B: I read somewhere that if you get up *energetic/energetically*, you'll feel good all day.

7 A: You came in rather *noisy/noisily* last night.

  B: Sorry, I didn't mean to be so *noisy/noisily*.

8 A: This exercise isn't very *hard/hardly*.

  B: No? Well, work *hard/hardly* to the end because the second part is difficult.

4 A Complete the sentences with adverbs formed from the adjectives in brackets.

1 You have to drive *carefully* (careful) and _____ (safe). You can't drive _____ (dangerous) or _____ (fast).

2 You have to work very _____ (hard) and often very _____ (late) at night but you get long summer holidays. You don't have to speak _____ (loud), but it helps.

3 You should eat _____ (healthy) and go to bed _____ (early). You don't have to walk or run _____ (fast), but you have to see _____ (clear).

4 You don't have to read music _____ (perfect), but it helps. You have to sing _____ (good), but you don't have to sing _____ (loud).

B What jobs are the sentences in Exercise 4A about? Underline the correct alternative.

1 a bus driver / a racing driver

2 a teacher / a politician

3 a footballer / a golfer

4 a jazz singer / an opera singer

5 Complete the adjectives and adverbs in the conversations.

Conversation 1

A: Are you OK?

B: No, I don't feel very we*ll*_____. Can I lie down somewhere?

A: Yes, over here.

B: I'm really tir_____. I slept terri_____ last night.

Conversation 2

A: This room's very comf_____.

B: Yes, but it's quite noi_____. I can hear the people downstairs.

A: Well, we don't have to stay here all evening. I'm hun_____.

B: Yes, we can eat che_____ in the café tonight and then we can go to that exp_____ Italian restaurant tomorrow.

Conversation 3

A: I sing very ba_____.

B: No, you don't. You sing beau_____.

A: Thank you. That's ki_____ of you.

WRITING

ADVERBS IN STORIES

6 A Write the adverbs.

1 slow   *slowly*
2 quick   _____
3 angry   _____
4 nervous   _____
5 careful   _____

B Complete the joke with the adverbs from Exercise 6A.

A *man walked* ¹ _nervously_ *into the dentist's office. The dentist looked* ² _____ *at the man's teeth and then said, 'I have to take one tooth out. I can do it* ³ _____ *– it'll only take five minutes and it'll cost $100.'*

'A hundred dollars for five minutes' work!' the man said ⁴ _____. *'That's too expensive!'*

'Well,' answered the dentist, 'I can do it ⁵ _____ *if you want!'*

VOCABULARY
VERBS OF MOVEMENT

1 Complete the conversations with the verbs in the box.

~~carry~~ drop lift stand cross push lie pick up

1 A: I'll take these dishes.
B: Don't _____carry_____ all of them. You'll _____ them!

2 A: Don't _____ the road now – the crossing light is still red.
B: Sorry, I didn't look.

3 A: And then my car just stopped.
B: So what did you do?
A: Lee helped me to _____ it – and a couple of minutes later, it started again.

4 A: Don't worry, I'll be OK. Oh, no!
B: What's the matter?
A: This box is too heavy. I can't _____ it!
B: I can _____ it _____ for you.

5 A: Don't _____ in the sun for too long. You'll get sunburnt.
B: Twenty minutes is not too long – I'll be fine.

6 A: Hi, Jenny. It's me.
B: Hi, Frank. Where are you?
A: I'm on the train. It's really crowded, so I have to _____.

FUNCTION
OFFERING TO HELP

2 A Put 1–4 and a)–d) in the correct order to make sentences.

1 my / problem / MP3 / there's / a / player / with
There's a problem with my MP3 player . ___

2 favourite / was / that / my / vase
_____. ___

3 tired / really / I'm
_____. ___

4 in / cold / here / it's
_____. ___

a) coffee / let / you / a / make / me
_____.

b) look / me / let
_____.

c) you / I'll / buy / one / another
_____.

d) I / window / shall / close / the
_____?

B Match sentences 1–4 in Exercise 2A with offers a)–d).

3 A Read Jim's 'To do' list. Then complete the conversation.

TO DO

- phone Noriko in Tokyo
- email Moscow office
- get flowers for Ellie – send them to hospital
- meet Anne at airport (5.30)

Ruth: Are you OK, Jim?
Jim: No. I have to meet Anne at 5.30 and look at this list!
Ruth: ¹ _Let_ me _help_ . I'm not busy at the moment.
Jim: Oh, can you? Thanks!
Ruth: No problem. ² _____ I _____ Noriko?
Jim: Yes, please.
Ruth: And then I ³ _____ _____ the Moscow office.
Jim: Can you tell them I'll phone tomorrow?
Ruth: OK. And I ⁴ _____ _____ some flowers for Ellie. I'm going to the hospital to see her tonight anyway.
Jim: Fantastic! ⁵ _____ me _____ you the money.
Ruth: It's OK. Give it to me tomorrow.
Jim: Thanks a lot. I ⁶ _____ _____ the same for you any time!

B ▶ 11.3 Listen and check. Then listen and repeat the offers of help.

LEARN TO
THANK SOMEONE

4 Circle the correct option.

1 A: Are you OK? Let me carry that.
B: a) Yes.   b) No problem.   **c)** Thanks a lot.

2 A: Shall I speak to Mr Chen for you?
B: a) That's kind of you.   b) You're welcome.   c) It's a problem.

3 A: I'll drive you home.
B: a) You're welcome.   b) Shall I do it?
   c) Thanks. I'm very grateful.

4 A: Thank you very much.
B: a) Yes.   b) You're welcome.   c) Your welcome.

5 A: Is this seat free?
B: Sure.
A: a) Thanks a lot.   b) No problem.   c) You're welcome.

6 A: I'll buy lunch.
B: a) Really? Please.   b) Really? Sure.   c) Really? Thanks.

VOCABULARY
EXPERIENCES

1 A Underline the correct alternative.

1 I'm very excited. I'm going to *do/be* in a play.
2 Look, we can *ride/drive* an elephant on a forest tour on Wednesday.
3 Let's *climb/do* Mount Bromo – it's a live volcano.
4 Are you really going to *make/do* the bungee jump?
5 Harry *met/saw* his new friend Ali on a train journey across Pakistan.
6 On Saturdays we *go to/play* a rugby match – we love watching sport.
7 *Sleeping/Meeting* outside? No, thank you – camping's not for me!
8 Come on, let's sit over there and *look/watch* the sun rise.

B ▶ **12.1** Listen and write the phrases in the correct column for each stress pattern.

1 ooO	2 oooO
	be in a play
3 ooOo	**4 ooOoo**

C Listen again and repeat.

WRITING
LINKERS REVIEW

2 Complete the email with the words in the box.

so	but	and	then	because	too	or	first
finally	as well						

Dear Mum and Dad,

We're having a great time. There's lots of snow,
¹___so___ skiing down the mountain is perfect.
The ski slopes are near ²_____ you can go ice-skating ³_____. The hotel's beautiful – a little
noisy ⁴_____ there's a big group staying here,
⁵_____ it's a lovely old building in the centre of
the village.

There are some famous people here. ⁶_____,
Karen met Justin Davies (he's a pop star, Mum!) at
breakfast and ⁷_____ I saw Emma Bower, the
pianist, on the ski slope. ⁸_____, in the evening
we did karaoke with Ercol Blonde, the rock star
from the 80s!

The food's great ⁹_____ – really tasty! Speaking
of food, it's dinner in five minutes, so
I must go now. I hope you're all OK. I'll call
¹⁰_____ email you again tomorrow!

Love, Janis

GRAMMAR
PRESENT PERFECT

3 Write the past participle of the verbs.

1 be   _been_   6 ride   _____
2 climb   _____   7 drink _____
3 do   _____   8 play   _____
4 travel _____   9 meet   _____
5 have   _____   10 fly   _____

4 A Look at the table and complete the sentences. Use the present perfect form of the verbs.

	Ethan	Amy	Tom and Lily
go to South America	✓	✗	✓
see Red Square	✗	✓	✓
eat Mexican food	✗	✓	✗
visit the Louvre gallery in Paris	✗	✗	✓
swim in the Black Sea	✓	✗	✗

1 Ethan ___has been___ to South America.
2 Amy _____ to South America.
3 Tom and Lily _____ Red Square.
4 Ethan _____ Red Square.
5 Amy _____ Mexican food.
6 Tom and Lily _____ Mexican food.
7 Tom and Lily _____ the Louvre gallery in Paris.
8 Amy _____ in the Black Sea.

B Complete the questions. Use the present perfect form of the verbs.

1 ___Has___ Ethan ___swum___ in the Black Sea?
2 _____ Ethan and Amy _____ the Louvre gallery in Paris?
3 _____ Lily _____ Mexican food?
4 _____ Amy _____ Red Square?
5 _____ Tom and Lily _____ to South America?
6 _____ Tom _____ in the Black Sea?

C Write short answers to questions 1–6 in Exercise 4B.

1 *Yes, he has.*
2 _____
3 _____
4 _____
5 _____
6 _____

READING

5 A Read Jim's travel blog and write the correct day under each picture.

A

Day 1

B

C

D

E

Day 1

We arrived in Piraeus early this morning. Liz has never seen the Parthenon. I've been to Athens once before, so I'm going to be her tour guide. We're going there tonight!

In the afternoon, we went by train from Piraeus into the city of Athens, and walked up to the Parthenon – amazing!

Day 2

Back to Athens again and this time we found a restaurant in the Plaka area. We've eaten Greek food many times back in New Zealand, but this is real Greek food! This is the first time in my life that I've tried octopus and it was delicious!

Day 3

We stayed overnight in Athens and then took a bus down to Cape Sounion in the afternoon to visit the Temple of Poseidon. We've seen many sunsets in our lives, but this was the most beautiful – the sun going down into the Aegean Sea.

Day 4

We left Piraeus early this morning and sailed for twenty hours to the island of Santorini. We arrived in the old port late in the evening. Tomorrow morning we're going up to the village – by donkey! I've ridden horses, camels, and elephants but I've never ridden a donkey!

Day 5

Donkey disaster! I'm writing this from a hospital bed in Athens. We started our donkey ride this morning and I made a big mistake: I walked behind the donkey and it kicked me in the stomach! There was no hospital on the island, so they took me by helicopter to Athens. I've broken three bones ... and I still haven't ridden a donkey. But I *have* flown in a helicopter!

B Read the blog again. Are the sentences true (T) or false (F)?

1 Jim and Liz walked from Piraeus to Athens.   *F*
2 Jim hasn't eaten Greek food before.   _____
3 Jim liked the octopus.   _____
4 They watched the sunrise near the Temple of Poseidon.   _____
5 Jim and Liz travelled to Santorini by boat.   _____
6 Jim enjoyed riding the donkey.   _____
7 Jim flew back to Athens.   _____
8 Now he's back home in New Zealand.   _____

C Correct the false sentences.

Jim and Liz went to Athens by train.
_____
_____
_____
_____

6 A Imagine it's before the holiday. Read the blog again and write short answers to the questions.

1 Has Liz ever seen the Parthenon?   *No, she hasn't.*
2 Has Jim ever been to Athens?   _____
3 Has Jim ever eaten octopus?   _____
4 Have Jim and Liz ever seen a sunset?   _____
5 Has Jim ever ridden a donkey?   _____

B Now imagine it's after the holiday. Read the questions in Exercise 6A again and write short answers.

1 *Yes, she has.*
2 _____
3 _____
4 _____
5 _____

LISTENING

1 A Match activities 1–8 with pictures A–H.

1 go on a roller coaster   *B*
2 get lost   _____
3 be on TV   _____
4 sing in a karaoke club   _____
5 go to the cinema alone   _____
6 fly in a helicopter   _____
7 swim in a lake   _____
8 drive in bad weather   _____

B Complete the quiz with the past participle of the verbs in brackets.

Have you ever ...

1   *been*   on a roller coaster? (go)

2   _____   lost in a city? (get)

3   _____   on TV? (be)

4   _____   in a karaoke club? (sing)

5   _____   to the cinema alone to see a film? (go)

6   _____   in a helicopter? (fly)

7   _____   in a lake? (swim)

8   _____   in really bad weather? (drive)

C ▶ 12.2 Listen to four conversations. Which situations from Exercise 1B do the people talk about?

Conversation 1   *6*
Conversation 2   _____
Conversation 3   _____
Conversation 4   _____

D Listen again. Write when the person did the activity.

Conversation 1   *five years ago*
Conversation 2   _____
Conversation 3   _____
Conversation 4   _____

GRAMMAR
PRESENT PERFECT AND PAST SIMPLE

2 Underline the correct alternatives.

Conversation 1

A: ¹*Did you ever fly/Have you ever flown* in a helicopter?

B: No, I ²*didn't/haven't.* ³*Did/Have* you?

A: Yes, I ⁴*did/have.* Just once, when I ⁵*went/'ve been* helicopter skiing, five years ago.

Conversation 2

A: ⁶*Have you ever sung/Did you ever sing* in a karaoke bar?

B: No, but I ⁷*sang/'ve sung* at a party. It ⁸*was/'s been* last year sometime. No, two years ago. At a birthday party.

A: What ⁹*did you sing/have you sung*?

B: I can't remember ... Oh, yes – *I did it my way.*

Conversation 3

A: ¹⁰*Did you ever drive/Have you ever driven* in really bad weather?

B: Yes. I ¹¹*drove/'ve driven* up to Scotland to visit my grandparents in 2007, and it just ¹²*snowed/has snowed* non-stop.

3 Complete the conversations with the present perfect or past simple form of the verbs in brackets.

Conversation 1

A: ¹*Have you ever ridden* (you / ever / ride) a horse?

B: Yes, I have. I ²_____ (ride) one in Argentina last year.

A: ³_____ (you / like) it?

B: Yes, it ⁴_____ (be) fun, but the horse ⁵_____ (not go) very fast.

Conversation 2

A: Does Emilio go everywhere by motorbike?

B: Yes, he does.

A: ⁶_____ (he / ever / hurt) himself?

B: Yes, he ⁷_____ (break) his arm twice.

A: Really? How ⁸_____ (he / do) that?

B: Both times the weather ⁹_____ (be) bad and he ¹⁰_____ (fall) off the bike.

VOCABULARY
PREPOSITIONS

4 Look at the map and complete the directions with the prepositions in the box.

| through (x2)   down   up   under   towards |
| away from   across   over   into |

Get off the train and walk ¹ _through_ the station and ²_____ the steps. There's a big square in front of the station with a clock tower on the other side. Walk ³_____ the square ⁴_____ the clock tower. Walk past the clock tower and go straight on until you see a bridge going ⁵_____ the road. Walk ⁶_____ the bridge and soon you'll see a shopping centre on your left. It's called WhiteWays. Walk ⁷_____ the shopping centre and at the other side you'll come out in Kirkby Street. Walk along Kirkby Street ⁸_____ the shopping centre. Then turn right into Sedgefield Road. My flat is in number thirty-five. The door's usually open so just come ⁹_____ the hall. Walk ¹⁰_____ the stairs to the first floor. My door is the blue one.

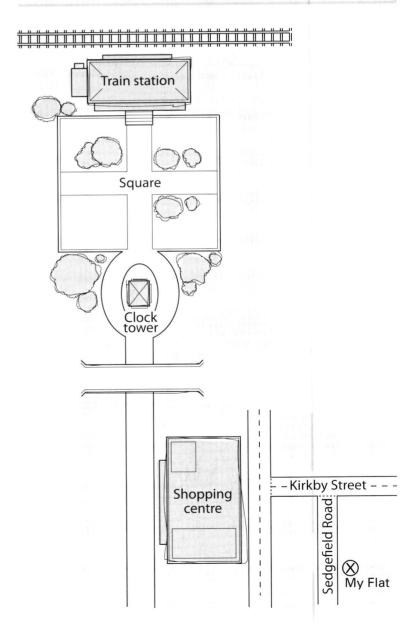

VOCABULARY

TELEPHONING EXPRESSIONS

1 Complete Susie's answerphone messages with verbs in the correct form.

1 This is Lisa from the health clinic. I *left*_____ a message on your answerphone yesterday. Can you p_____ the clinic, please?

2 Hi, Susie. It's Meg. Can you r_____ me back? I'm at home this evening.

3 Hi. It's me, Bernie. Did you t_____ a message for me last night from Simon?

4 Hello. This is Sports Mad. Can you c_____ us, please? There's a problem with your trainers.

5 Hi, Susie. It's Fallon. I got your message and I'm ph_____ you back.

6 Hi, it's me again. I know you're there! A_____ the phone!

FUNCTION

TELEPHONING

2 Find and correct mistakes in six of the sentences. Tick the two correct sentences.

       her
1 Just ask ~~she~~ to call me.

2 Could you say me the number?

3 OK, I ring you back.

4 Could I leave a message to her?

5 Let me check that.

6 Hi, Frank. I'm Sally.

7 Good morning. Could I chat to Mr Suriano, please?

8 Just a moment.

3 Write telephone conversations using the prompts.

Conversation 1

A: could / ring / me / back, please?
_____

B: Of course. / can / you / give / number?
_____

A: yes, / it / 0141 6493861
_____

B: let / check / that. / 0141 6493861
_____

A: that / right
_____

Conversation 2

A: Hi, Xavier. This / Bea
Hi, Xavier. This is Bea.

B: Hi, Bea. How / you?
_____

A: I / OK. Michelle / there?
_____

B: Yes, but she / sleep
_____

A: I / leave / message / her?
_____

B: Of course.
A: just ask / to call / me
_____

B: OK. Bye.

Conversation 3

A: Hello. / I / speak / the manager, please?

B: just / moment. I / sorry, he / busy / moment. / call / back later?
_____

A: it / very important
_____

B: I / take / message?
_____

A: no thanks / I / phone back later
_____

LEARN TO

SAY TELEPHONE NUMBERS

4 A Write the telephone numbers in words. Put a comma between number groups.

1 3234996 *three two three, four double nine six*
2 6882975 _____
3 0757281 _____
4 6232889 _____
5 9897766 _____
6 0870 5338992 _____
_____

B ▶ 12.3 Listen and check. Then listen and repeat.

GRAMMAR VERB FORMS

1 A Complete the article with the correct form of the verbs in brackets. Use the past simple, the present perfect, *would like to* or *be going to*.

Irish nurse Liz Johnson works with the international aid agency, Médecins Sans Frontières (MSF). She talked to us about her experiences.

'About seven years ago I ¹ _saw_ (see) a TV programme about MSF and I ² _____ (decide) to work for them. I ³ _____ (join) MSF three months later.'

'I love my work. I ⁴ _____ (go) to a lot of different places in the world and I ⁵ _____ (meet) some amazing people: doctors, nurses, helpers and patients. In fact, four years ago in Sudan I ⁶ _____ (meet) my husband, Jacques, a French doctor. We now travel and work together. I'm very proud of him.'

Last week Liz and Jacques ⁷ _____ (return) to France after six months work in Haiti. What are their plans for the future? 'We've got some definite plans: Jacques ⁸ _____ (speak) at a big MSF meeting next week and then we ⁹ _____ (have) a one-week holiday in Spain. After that we aren't sure. Next, we ¹⁰ _____ (open) a hospital, but we don't know in which country.'

B Put the words in the correct order to make questions for Liz.

1 did / decide / you / for / when / to / MSF / work
When did you decide to work for MSF ?

2 you / to / a / have / been / lot / different / of / countries
_____?

3 meet / you / husband / did / when / your
_____?

4 to / Jacques / going / week / where / speak / is / next
_____?

5 do / you / like / to / next / would / what
_____?

C Now imagine you are Liz. Answer the questions.

1 *About seven years ago.* _____
2 _____
3 _____
4 _____
5 _____

VOCABULARY REVISION

2 A Add vowels to the words in each group.

1
f i n a lly
_ s w _ ll
b _ c _ _ s _
_ ls _
first

2
h _ _ d _ ch _
s _ r _ thr _ _ t
t _ mp _ r _ t _ r _
c _ _ gh
_____

3
thr _ _ gh
t _ w _ rds
_ w _ y fr _ m
_ _ t _ f
_____

4
h _ ngry
th _ rsty
s _ nb _ rnt
l _ st
_____

5
dr _ w _ ng
c _ nc _ rt
_ xh _ b _ t _ _ n
st _ t _ _ _

6
c _ rry
dr _ p
l _ ft
p _ ck _ p
_____

7
sh _ _ ld _ r
kn _ _
f _ ng _ r
_ lb _ w
_____

B Match headings a)–g) with groups 1–7 in Exercise 2A.

a) linkers ____1____
b) the body _____
c) health _____
d) art and culture _____
e) prepositions of movement _____
f) verbs of movement _____
g) words that go with *get* _____

C Add the words in the box to the groups in Exercise 2A. There are two extra words.

~~first~~ stung conversation into runny nose
dance performance neck text message push

GRAMMAR　SHOULD/WILL/MIGHT

3 A　Read the text. Who has these problems? Daniel (D), Rebecca (R) or both (DR)?

1　wants to change jobs　　　　_R_
2　works too much　　　　____
3　lives unhealthily　　　　____
4　doesn't have any friends　　____
5　is bored with work　　　　____
6　has money problems　　　____

life coaching*

Improve your life and reach your dreams …

Read about two of our customers and how life coaching has helped them:

Daniel is a successful businessman, but he finds it difficult to make friends so at weekends he stays at home and spends a lot of time alone on his computer. On weekdays, he often stays in the office late. He's also overweight and says he's never done much exercise. He'd like to become healthier and go out and meet people, maybe find a girlfriend, but he doesn't know where to start.

Rebecca loves dancing and she teaches a dance class once a week. She works for an electronics company, but she doesn't like her job. She thinks it's boring and works long hours, but she needs the money because her rent is very high. She'd like to teach dance all the time, but she doesn't know how to start.

*coaching = training, teaching

B　Read the life-coaching advice and underline the correct alternatives.

Daniel ¹_should_/'ll look for activities he can do with other people. He ²should/shouldn't join a club or group, for example a walking club or a cooking group because then he ³'ll/might meet people who enjoy the same things. When he's with other people he ⁴should/shouldn't ask them lots of questions and he ⁵should/shouldn't show interest in their answers. People love talking about themselves and they ⁶'ll/won't think he's a great guy! Who knows? He ⁷'ll/might find a girlfriend one day!

Rebecca ⁸shouldn't/might not wait any more. She's in the wrong job. She ⁹should/'ll contact the Association of Dance Teachers – she can find them on the internet and they ¹⁰might/'ll give her advice about starting a new business. At the moment she ¹¹won't/shouldn't leave her job. The best thing is to work part-time, but her company ¹²might/might not agree. She ¹³should/shouldn't start teaching more classes – lots of people want to learn to dance and I'm sure she ¹⁴won't/might not find it difficult to reach her dream.

VOCABULARY　PLANS

4　Find twelve verb phrases for future plans in the puzzle.

W	T	R	G	R	W	Y	H	T	H
H	O	V	E	A	B	H	I	A	D
A	I	S	T	A	Y	I	N	K	O
V	U	G	M	V	G	D	M	E	S
E	G	O	A	N	O	O	O	A	O
A	O	S	R	G	J	A	V	B	M
B	F	H	R	G	O	C	E	R	E
A	O	O	I	G	G	O	H	E	W
R	R	P	E	I	G	U	O	A	O
B	A	P	D	C	I	R	M	K	R
E	W	I	L	R	N	S	E	V	K
C	A	N	A	Z	G	E	B	E	T
U	L	G	E	T	A	J	O	B	B
E	K	Q	S	C	K	X	L	L	X
G	O	F	O	R	A	M	E	A	L

FUNCTION　TELEPHONING, OFFERING AND SUGGESTING

5 A　Complete the poem.

'Could I ¹_speak_____to Susie Dee?'
'She's not at ²h_____. She's back at three.
Could you ³p_____ her back tonight?'
'I'll ⁴l_____ a message. Is that all right?'
'Just a ⁵m_____, I need a pen.'
'She's got my ⁶n_____. My name's Ben.'
'⁷L_____ me check – your name is Jack?'
'Oh, never mind – I'll ⁸c_____ her back.'

'Well, hello Susie! How are you?'
'I'm fine. What ⁹w_____ you like to do?'
'Why ¹⁰d_____ we meet and have a chat?'
'I don't really ¹¹f_____ like doing that.'
'Then how ¹²a_____ a walk together?'
'¹³S_____ good. Let me check the weather.
It's going to rain – that's not ideal.'
'So ¹⁵l_____ stay in and cook a meal!'

B　▶ R4.1　Listen and check.

CHECK

Circle the correct option to complete the sentences.

1 You dance _____.
   a) beautiful   **b)** good   **c)** well

2 **A:** It's Estelle's birthday on Saturday.
   B: Yes, _____ her a camera. I ordered it last week.
   a) I'm going to give   **b)** I'd like to give   **c)** I give

3 **A:** Should I tell Felipe?
   B: _____
   a) Yes, you should tell.   **b)** No, you shouldn't.
   c) Yes, you shouldn't.

4 Mack ran quickly _____ Anya and said, 'I'm so happy to see you!'
   a) away from   **b)** towards   **c)** across

5 Jan _____ to Germany.
   a) never has been   **b)** was never   **c)** has never been

6 I've got _____.
   a) the headache   **b)** a cough   **c)** my sore throat

7 Have you ever _____ in a lake?
   a) swim   **b)** swam   **c)** swum

8 **A:** Oh, no! A snake!
   B: Don't be afraid. I'm sure it _____ you.
   a) won't hurt   **b)** 'll hurt   **c)** might not

9 Hi, _____ Fabio. Is Luigi there?
   a) I'm   **b)** this is   **c)** is this

10 **A:** I feel worse today.
   B: You _____.
   a) should to go home   **b)** shouldn't go to bed
   c) should go to bed

11 **A:** Where _____ in Malta?
   B: At the Carlton Hotel.
   a) you're going to stay   **b)** are you going to stay
   c) you would like to stay

12 They _____ yesterday.
   a) 've been fishing   **b)** 've gone fishing
   c) went fishing

13 Peter's very _____ today.
   a) seriously   **b)** quiet   **c)** noisily

14 We _____ a great barbecue – about twenty people came.
   a) went   **b)** had   **c)** got

15 **A:** Tom Grady has got a temperature and he _____ says his arms and legs hurt.
   B: I'll phone his mother. I think he's got flu.
   a) also   **b)** too   **c)** as well

16 He jumped out of _____.
   a) a helicopter   **b)** a bridge   **c)** an elephant

17 It's not easy for me to _____ a conversation in Spanish.
   a) make   **b)** have   **c)** do

18 I always carry lots of water with me so I don't get _____.
   a) dry   **b)** thirsty   **c)** hungry

19 Sorry, I can't talk at the moment. Can I _____ in half an hour?
   a) leave a message   **b)** take a message
   c) phone you back

20 I love *The Great Gatsby*. I _____ it about ten times.
   a) saw   **b)** see   **c)** 've seen

21 My _____ hurts.
   a) shoulder   **b)** flu   **c)** temperature

22 You have to go _____ passport control and security.
   a) out of   **b)** through   **c)** into

23 He drove _____ through the city.
   a) fastly   **b)** slow   **c)** fast

24 **A:** What shall we do tonight?
   B: _____ stay in and watch a DVD.
   a) Let's   **b)** Why we don't   **c)** How about

25 **A:** Did Jake invite you to his wedding?
   B: Yes, but I _____ go because it's in Canada and it's very expensive to fly there.
   a) might   **b)** might not   **c)** 'll

26 _____ that for you?
   a) Let me carry   **b)** Shall I carry   **c)** I'll carry

27 Have you ever been to China?
   a) No, I haven't.   **b)** Yes, I have been to.
   c) Yes, I have gone.

28 We _____ get married!
   a) going to   **b)** 're going to   **c)** 're going

29 I hurt my _____ yesterday and I can't walk.
   a) thumb   **b)** finger   **c)** toe

30 I _____ around the world.
   a) 'd like to travel   **b)** 'm like to travel
   c) like travel

RESULT   **/30**

UNIT 1 Recording 1

1 German, Russian, Mexican, Canadian
2 Polish, Spanish, Scottish
3 Portuguese, Chinese, Japanese
4 Greek, Thai

UNIT 1 Recording 2

keys
mobile phone
passport
sunglasses
sweater
diary
magazine
laptop
newspaper
watch
ticket
camera

UNIT 1 Recording 3

I = Interviewer   P = Passenger

I: Hello and welcome to *The Travel Programme*. We're at Heathrow Airport in London to ask people about their bags. What's in their hand luggage?

…

I: Excuse me, sir. Do you have a moment?
P1: Oh, er, yes. OK.
I: Can I ask you a couple of questions? First of all, where are you from?
P1: I'm from Germany.
I: And are you here on business or are you a tourist?
P1: I'm here on business.
I: And can I ask you – what's in your bag?
P1: In my bag? Um, let's see. It's a small bag, so not very much. My passport and plane ticket, my mobile phone and … let's see … yes, and keys. That's all.
I: Thank you very much.

…

I: Excuse me, can I ask you a couple of questions? It's for the radio.
P2: The radio? Oh, OK.
I: Right. Where are you from?
P2: I'm American.
I: And are you here on business?
P2: No, no, I'm just a tourist.
I: And can I ask you – what's in your bag today?
P2: That's a strange question! OK, er, a camera, a newspaper from home – from L.A. – my sunglasses, my MP3 player and earphones … Um, that's it.
I: And your passport?
P2: It's here in my pocket. My passport, credit cards and money are never in my bag.
I: Thanks very much.

…

I: Excuse me, where are you from?
P3: I'm French. Why?
I: It's for a radio programme. Are you here on business?
P3: Yes, yes, on business.
I: And what's in your bag?
P3: My bag? Oh, OK. My mobile, my laptop, a magazine, sunglasses, my passport and ticket, and my diary. That's it.
I: Thank you.

UNIT 1 Recording 4

1 These glasses are mine.
2 These keys are yours.
3 That bag is Jack's.
4 Those pencils are mine.
5 This mobile phone is Anita's.
6 That magazine is yours.

UNIT 1 Recording 5

1 Could I have one of those postcards, please?
2 Can I have a return ticket to Paris, please?
3 Can I have a cheese sandwich, please?
4 Could I have a tea and a coffee, please?
5 Can I have those sunglasses, please?

UNIT 1 Recording 6

1 **A:** How much is a coffee cake, please?
  B: It's two euros.
2 **A:** Could I have a return to Sydney, please?
  B: That's ten fifty.
3 **A:** Is that a cheese sandwich?
  B: No, it's a chicken sandwich.
4 **A:** That's eight euros, please.
  B: Ah, I only have six euros.

UNIT 1 Recording 7

A: Hello.
B: Hello. Can I have a tomato salad and a mineral water, please?
A: That's two euros for the salad and one euro for the mineral water.
B: Thanks.
A: Anything else?
B: Er, how much is an ice cream?
A: One euro fifty cents.
B: OK. Can I have an ice cream, too?
C: Hi. How much are the sandwiches?
A: Which ones?
C: The egg and the chicken.
A: The egg is two euros seventy cents and the chicken is three fifty.
C: And a cheese sandwich?
A: That's two twenty.
C: OK. Can I have two cheese sandwiches and a chicken sandwich, please?
A: Anything to drink?
C: Er … yes, three coffees, please.
A: Three coffees at one fifty each. OK, so, that's four forty for the cheese sandwiches, three fifty for the chicken sandwich, and another four fifty for the coffees. That's twelve euros and forty cents altogether.
C: Here you are.

UNIT 2 Recording 1

game
newspaper
sport
magazine
coffee
cinema
exercise
MP3 player
DVD
TV
nothing
film
tennis
pasta
fun

UNIT 2 Recording 2

A: Can I help you?
B: Yes, hi. I'm interested in one of your courses.
A: OK. Which course do you want to do?
B: Er, I don't know. Can you help me?
A: Sure. Well, do you like music?
B: Yes, I do. I listen to music a lot at home, and … I sing in the car sometimes.
A: Then maybe Singing for fun? The class is on Monday and Thursday evenings from six-thirty till eight-thirty at the music school.
B: And what do they do in the classes?
A: Well, the teachers play the guitar and the students er, sing – old songs, new songs. They, er …
B: I'm not sure. No, I don't think that's good for me.
A: OK. Let's see … Do you take photos?
B: Well, I take them on holiday.
A: Because the Digital photography course is on Saturday mornings from nine to twelve at the high school. A good time if you work Monday to Friday. You study how to take good photos. The teacher is a photographer.
B: Hmm … no, no, I don't like photography much.
A: Well, do you like dancing? There's a salsa group – Salsa for beginners. They meet at the dance club on Tuesdays and Thursdays from seven to nine and practise salsa dancing. I know that at the weekend they meet and go to dance clubs.

B: Oh, no. I don't dance.

A: Hmm. OK. Where do you work?

B: At a bank.

A: And do you sit at your desk a lot?

B: Yes, all day. I don't do much exercise.

A: Yes, me too. I'm here all day on the computer, but I do Office yoga.

B: What do you do in an Office yoga class?

A: Oh, it's great! We meet here at Union County on Mondays and Wednesdays from seven thirty to nine. We learn exercises that you do at your desk – stretching and relaxing exercises.

B: Yeah. That's good. Er, yes … OK, OK. Office yoga. How much is it? And when are the classes …

UNIT 2 Recording 3

1 /s/: sleeps, drinks, eats, gets
2 /z/: plays, drives, studies, knows, leaves
3 /ɪz/: relaxes, washes, practises

UNIT 2 Recording 4

1 What time does the train leave?
2 When does the train arrive?
3 What time does the tour start?
4 When does the tour finish?
5 Where does the tour start from?
6 How much does the tour cost?
7 What time does the bank open?
8 When does the bank close?

UNIT 2 Recording 5

1

A: Hello, National Rail. Can I help you?

B: Yes, I want to go from London to Cambridge this morning. What time does the next train leave?

A: There's one at 10.52, getting into Cambridge at 11.54.

B: Sorry, could you speak more slowly please? What time does it leave?

A: 10.52.

B: 10.52. That's soon. Er, what time's the next train after that?

A: The next one leaves at 11.15.

B: And when does it arrive in Cambridge?

A: At 12.10.

B: 12.10. Great. Thank you.

2

A: Hello.

B: Hello, can I help you?

A: Yes, can you tell me about the Bangkok Temple Tour?

B: OK.

A: Er, what time does it start?

B: It starts at 7a.m.

A: 7a.m! That's early. When does it finish?

B: Lunchtime. At about 1 o'clock.

A: OK. And where does it start from?

B: Oh, it starts and ends at the Wat Phra Kaew.

A: Excuse me, the Wat Phra … Er, could you spell that?

B: Sure. W-A-T P-H-R-A K-A-E-W.

A: Thanks.

B: Would you like to book the tour?

A: How much does it cost?

B: Six hundred and fifty baht.

A: How much is that in euros?

B: Fourteen euros.

A: OK, yes, please.

3

A: Hello, National Bank. Can I help you?

B: Yes, just a question about your opening hours. What time do you open on Monday?

A: We open at 9.30 on Monday to Friday.

B: Sorry, could you repeat that? Nine …?

A: Half past nine.

B: And what time do you close?

A: At four.

B: Are you open on Saturdays?

A: Yes, from 10a.m.

B: And what time do you close?

A: At 1p.m.

B: OK, thank you.

UNIT 3 Recording 1

1 sister, mother
2 cousin, uncle
3 wife, niece
4 aunt, father
5 son, husband
6 grandfather, parents
7 daughter, brother
8 nephew, friend

UNIT 3 Recording 2

M = Meg   D = David

M: OK, Tom. Nice to talk to you. Bye!

D: So who was that?

M: My brother, Tom.

D: Oh, have you got a lot of brothers and sisters?

M: No, just one brother and one sister. Tom and Candy.

D: Uh huh. Do you see them a lot?

M: Well, Tom and I are very close. We often do things together – go to the cinema, play tennis … but I don't see Candy very often. She lives in Scotland and we aren't very close. How about you, David?

D: I'm from a big family. I've got five brothers and a sister.

M: Five! That's a lot of brothers!

D: Yeah, but I don't see them often. Four of them live a long way away. Nick lives here in the city but we hardly ever meet.

M: Why not?

D: Well, he's quite serious and quiet and … well, we like doing different things. He likes staying at home and reading and I … I'm quite active and I like going out.

M: Oh, I see. It's the same for me and Candy. She doesn't like going out and she isn't very talkative.

D: That makes telephoning a bit difficult.

M: Yeah. So what about *your* sister?

D: Oh, Jenny and I, we're good friends. We're close. I talk to her a lot. She phones me every day for a chat – usually about *her* problems.

M: Yeah?

D: Well, she's got a difficult family situation. Her husband hasn't got a job, they've got three children, no money – you know.

M: Oh. How old are the children?

D: They're very young – two, five and seven. All boys.

M: Wow, three young kids and no money! That's hard.

D: Yes, so we never talk about *my* life.

M: So she doesn't know about your new job?

D: No, she thinks I'm still a waiter!

M: But you have this great job now! You have to tell her. She's your sister, she'll be happy.

D: Maybe you're right. I don't know, I feel uncomfortable. Ah, that's my phone.

M: Who is it?

D: Oh, it's my sister! Hold on. Hi, Jenny. How are you?

UNIT 3 Recording 3

1 kind
2 funny, friendly, stupid, quiet, boring
3 unkind
4 talkative, serious, interesting
5 unfriendly
6 intelligent

REVIEW 1 Recording 1

1 finish, sweater, camera, Poland, Irish, waiter
2 newspaper, hairdresser, listen to, credit card, Canada, Mexican
3 Colombia, umbrella, accountant, do nothing, adaptor, Korean
4 engineer, souvenir, go to bed, Vietnam, magazine, Portuguese

REVIEW 1 Recording 2

1
I don't like my mobile phone.
I often want to be alone.
But then my mobile phone, it rings.
I really do not like these things!

2
A: What time does the train leave, please?
B: At half past four. Here, take these.
A: Two single tickets? Are they for me?
B: Yes, for five euros – they're not for free!

3
A: Could I have a sandwich, please?
B: Of course, what kind? Meat or cheese?
A: Oh, I'm not sure, so can I please have one of those and one of these?

4
A: Are you free at half past five?
B: No, sorry, that's when my friends arrive.
A: Then how about meeting at three?
B: Sorry, I'm busy.
A: When *are* you free?

REVIEW 1 Recording 3

R = Receptionist   G = Guest

R: Can I help you?
G: Hello. My, er, wallet. I, er, …
R: Oh, you've lost your wallet? Where did you have it last?
G: I'm sorry, I don't understand. Er, in the restaurant … I, er, …
R: No problem. Let me see. What colour is it?
G: Colour? Ah, it's, er, brown.
R: And how much money is there in the wallet?
G: Sorry. Could you speak more slowly, please?
R: Erm … how much money is in the wallet?
G: Ah, a hundred dollars and, er, my credit card.
R: OK, let me look. Is this yours?
G: No, no. My wallet's a different brown. Oh, that's mine! Yes, in the box!
R: OK, sir. Just a moment. I want to be sure that it's *your* wallet.
G: Of course it's my wallet!
R: Can you tell me anything that's in the wallet?
G: Sorry, could you repeat that?
R: What else is in the wallet?
G: Oh, er, a photo of my wife.
R: OK.
G: And some money and a credit card.
R: OK. This *is* yours.
G: Thank you!
R: Sorry, just a moment. I need to write some details for our records. Your name is …?

G: Moretti, Vincenzo Moretti.
R: That's M-O-double R?
G: No, one R and double T.
R: M-O-R-E-T-T-I … And your room number, Mr Moretti?
G: 368.
R: Have you got a mobile phone number?
G: Yes, it's 03837 4025.
R: … 4125.
G: No, 4025.
R: OK, thank you. Please sign here.
G: All right. Oh, what's the date?
R: Today's the ninth of April.
G: Ninth … April … OK, thank you very much!
R: Mr. Moretti?
G: Yes?
R: Is this your keycard?
G: Oh, ah yes! Thank you!

UNIT 4 Recording 1

1 Is there a <u>living</u> room?
2 There's a big <u>kitchen</u>.
3 Is there a <u>television</u>?
4 How many <u>people</u> are there?
5 There are <u>two</u> of us.
6 There's a large <u>shopping</u> centre.

UNIT 4 Recording 2

Here we are outside St Paul's Cathedral for our walking tour. On our way, we see the Museum of London, the Barbican Arts Centre, the Bank of England and the Monument to the Great Fire of London. Let's walk down St Martin's Le-Grand and to the Museum of London.

We're going into the Museum of London now – you can see very old jewellery from around 400 years ago here. Let's go in.

Next stop is the Barbican. We walk down London Wall and turn left at Wood Street. The Barbican is here – it's one of London's famous arts centres. You can see a play in the theatre or you can watch a film in the cinema.

Let's walk down Fore Street and turn right at Moorgate. Here you can find lots of supermarkets. You can buy food and also find restaurants for something to eat. Anyone hungry?

Let's go down Prince's Street now. On the left is Threadneedle Street. You can see the Old Lady of Threadneedle Street here – that's what we call the Bank of England. Now let's walk down King William Street to the Monument.

This is the Monument to the Great Fire of London. It's sixty-one metres high – you can climb to the top. At the top you can see all of London. There's also a post office just over there, so you can send your family and friends a postcard. OK, now let's …

UNIT 5 Recording 1

1 milk, chicken
2 fish, garlic
3 salad, apple
4 pepper, cheese
5 onions, noodles
6 banana, grapes
7 lettuce, butter
8 juice, fruit

UNIT 5 Recording 2

I = Interviewer   M = Mike

I: Welcome to *Twenty-four Seven*, the programme about people and lifestyle. Today we're talking to Dr Mike McKay, who wrote the bestseller *The Junk Food Lover's Diet*. So Dr McKay, is it true that on your diet I can eat anything I want?
M: Yes, that's right.
I: I can eat junk food – hamburgers, pizza, chocolate?
M: It's all fine. You can eat anything you want and you'll lose weight.
I: Well, can you explain that?
M: It's very simple. You can eat anything, but you can't eat a lot. So go ahead, get a hamburger every week – but don't eat the whole thing! Eat *half* of it.
I: Oh, I see. So with chocolate, for example, how much is enough? I love chocolate milk!
M: Well, one glass of chocolate milk a day is a lot. On the Junk Food Lover's Diet, you can drink three glasses a week – no more.
I: This sounds great! How about pizza? How much pizza is OK on the Junk Food Lover's Diet?
M: For lunch, you can have one piece of pizza.
I: Every day?
M: Every day.
I: I usually eat four or five!
M: Well, you can't eat that much. One piece a day – seven a week – is enough! On the Junk Food Lover's Diet, you can eat anything, but not a lot of one thing.
I: Is it OK to have pizza for dinner?
M: Well, pizza is very rich, so have pizza at lunchtime and eat light foods for dinner.
I: OK, how about biscuits?
M: Well, one packet of biscuits every day – you can't eat that, of course! But you can have two packets in a week.
I: So Monday and Wednesday are biscuit days!
M: Oh, OK!
I: How much ice cream can I eat?
M: One small bowl.
I: One bowl a day? That's not bad!

M: One a *week*! You can have one *small* bowl of ice cream a week – no more!

I: And a diet cola?

M: Or a regular cola.

I: Really? Cola with sugar?

M: Yup, but …

I: … only one can a week!

UNIT 5 Recording 3

1 I'd like a hamburger with onion and tomato and some salad, please.
2 Could I have a chicken sandwich with corn on the cob? And some onions on the sandwich, please. And some fries.
3 Can I have a hamburger with lettuce and onion? And a salad too, please.

UNIT 5 Recording 4

1 a hamburger with onion and tomato
2 could I have a chicken sandwich
3 corn on the cob
4 onions on the sandwich
5 lettuce and onion
6 and a salad too, please

UNIT 6 Recording 1

the nineteenth of March, nineteen fifty-nine
October the thirtieth, nineteen ninety-five
the thirty-first of March, two thousand and two
January the sixth, eighteen oh five
the thirteenth of October, nineteen fifty-seven
the twenty-first of May, nineteen ten
January the twenty-sixth, two thousand and five

UNIT 6 Recording 2

/t/:   worked, finished, stopped, helped
/d/:   changed, loved, played, tried, enjoyed, travelled
/ɪd/:   started, wanted, hated

UNIT 6 Recording 3

thought, met, spoke, grew, woke, taught, knew, drew, wrote, slept, left, bought

UNIT 6 Recording 4

P = Philip   **D** = Denise

P: Well, we didn't have any children, so we adopted Zsilan seven years ago. We went to China and we met Zsilan there – and we brought her home with us to Sydney. She was about two years old, but at first there was a problem.

D: Yes, she was a very intelligent little girl, but at first she was also really quiet. She ate a lot, but she didn't talk much, so we didn't know what to do.

P: Yes, she was very unhappy.

D: So we went on the internet and we looked for other families with adopted Chinese children. And we found a website and … well, we got a big surprise!

P: Yes, we wrote about Zsilan on the website. We wrote about her birthday – that it was on May the eighth …

D: And a woman in Melbourne wrote back to say that *her* daughter, also a Chinese girl, named Lin, had the same birthday!

P: So we put a photo of Zsilan on the website and this other woman put up a photo of Lin, and …

D: Here are the photos. Look at them! The girls look exactly the same!

P: Yes, so we started to think, 'Yes, maybe they are sisters; maybe they're twins. So we went to Melbourne with Zsilan and the two little girls met.

D: It was amazing, from the first moment! They looked at each other with such love and then they laughed and played together all day.

P: For the first time, I felt that Zsilan was really happy.

D: We were sorry to leave. Zsilan and Lin never lived together but they visit each other a lot and they like the same things: dancing and swimming …

P: A year ago, we had tests. And it was true – they *are* sisters! And with the same birthday, of course – they're twins.

D: When we told Zsilan that Lin really was her sister, she smiled and said, 'I *know* she's my sister.'

UNIT 6 Recording 5

1 **A:** What did you do on Saturday?
   B: I had lunch with my grandparents.
   A: That sounds nice.
2 **A:** Did you have a good day yesterday?
   B: No, we went for a walk and it rained!
   A: So what did you do?
3 **A:** Did you have a good weekend?
   B: I wasn't very well, so I stayed in bed.
   A: That sounds awful!
4 **A:** How was your weekend?
   B: Fantastic, thanks!
   A: Why, what did you do?
5 **A:** Did you do anything special at the weekend?
   B: No, we just stayed at home and relaxed.
   A: That sounds lovely.

REVIEW 2 Recording 1

1 The oranges are next to the bread.
2 The cheese is between the beans and the pasta.
3 The pasta is under the rice.
4 The apples are on the left of the oranges.
5 The grapes are behind the carrots.
6 The bread is above the grapes and carrots.
7 The apples are between the rice and the oranges.
8 The beans are on the left of the carrots.

UNIT 7 Recording 1

empty
noisy
cheap
boring
uncomfortable
slow
expensive
quiet
fast
comfortable
crowded
interesting

UNIT 7 Recording 2

Hello. It's 9.48a.m. on Monday the second of December. I'm Nick Young and I'm on the Trans-Siberian train. Welcome to my audio diary. First of all, some facts: the Trans-Siberian is the longest train journey in the world. It's nine thousand three hundred kilometres and takes seven days. So, this is day one. We left the city an hour ago and I'm here in my compartment. It's quite comfortable with two beds, one for me and one for Anton. Anton's from Sweden and he's very friendly. He doesn't speak much English, but that's not a problem.

…

Hi, Nick here. It's day three and we're in Siberia. Out of the window you can see snow and forests and small villages for kilometre after kilometre. It's beautiful. About every two hours the train stops at a small station and there are women selling bread, fish, fruit or vegetables. We often buy food for lunch or dinner. When we get back on the train, we chat and read and have more cups of tea. Then we have lunch and then dinner and then we go to bed. It's all very relaxing.

…

Hi there. This is my last audio diary on this journey. In one hour we get into Vladivostok station! Last night the Russian lady in the carriage next door had her fiftieth birthday party. It was crowded, but we had a good time! So what do I think about the Trans-Siberian train? Fantastic! And my best memories? Great dark forests, small Russian villages, and some good new friends. I really think this is the best journey of my life!

UNIT 7   Recording 3

1   **A:** So, the park's between the cinema and the pharmacy.
    B: No, it's behind the cinema and the pharmacy.
2   **A:** So, the supermarket's between the cinema and the pharmacy.
    B: No, it's between the cinema and the post office.
3   **A:** So, the cinema is the fourth building on the left.
    B: No, it's the third building on the left.
4   **A:** So, the café is the fourth building on the left.
    B: No, it's the fourth building on the right.
5   **A:** So, the post office is opposite the bank.
    B: No, it's opposite the museum.
6   **A:** So, the town hall is opposite the bank.
    B: No, it's next to the bank.

UNIT 8   Recording 1

1   Hello? Oh hi, Rob. No, we're at the new exhibition at the National Gallery and we're looking at the Klimt paintings. Yeah, they're fantastic. OK, see you later.
2   Nellie, it's me, Russ. Hi, yeah, we're queuing to buy tickets for the concert. Do you want to come? I can get you a ticket. Two? Oh, who's your new friend? Right. See you soon.
3   Hi. Oh, look, I can't talk now – we're just going into a concert. It's the Mozart. Yes, the *Requiem*. Sorry, I've got to go.
4   Hi, Felicity. Fine, thanks. Listen, do you want to have a coffee later? After the match – maybe around four o'clock. Yeah, it's Nadal again – he's amazing! Oh you're watching the match on TV? Right, see you at four.
5   Zsuzsa, I just had to call you. The new designs, they're fantastic – everything's black and white, you know. Kate's wearing white and Fabio's in all-black – black jeans, a black sweater and black jacket. OK, yeah, I'll take some pictures. Talk to you later.

UNIT 8   Recording 2

1   Are you looking for a film?
2   Is it an action film?
3   Is anyone famous in it?
4   Do you want to watch a film?
5   I haven't got a DVD player.
6   I've got it on my computer.

UNIT 8   Recording 3

1   Are you looking for a friend?
2   Is it an action film?
3   Is anyone famous in it?
4   Do you want to buy a DVD?
5   I haven't got a CD player.

UNIT 9   Recording 1

1   fast
2   healthy
3   dangerous
4   inconvenient
5   difficult
6   convenient
7   safe
8   easy
9   comfortable
10 polluting

UNIT 9   Recording 2

R = Reporter   C = Carin

R: We're in Amsterdam, the Netherlands, and we're talking to Carin van Buren. Carin's riding a kind of scooter with a motor. Carin, what is this, er, machine called?
C: It's a balancing scooter.
R: And do you ride it around the city?
C: Yes, I use it to go to work. Before this year I went to work by bike or sometimes by bus. Then I saw a balancing scooter on the internet and thought, 'That looks good,' and I bought one!
R: Is it difficult to ride?
C: No, it's actually very easy.
R: And how long does it take to learn to ride?
C: It takes about two hours. Yes, it took me two hours.
R: Can you ride it on the pavement here?
C: No, you can't. You have to ride it on the road or you can use the bike paths.
R: And how fast does it go?
C: The maximum speed is twenty-five kilometres an hour but I usually go slower than that.
R: Do you feel safe on it?
C: Yeah – yes, I do. I always wear a helmet. The scooter doesn't go very fast and it's easy to stop.
R: And is it better than travelling by bus or bike?
C: I think so. By bus it took about forty-five minutes to go to work and now it takes me twenty minutes by scooter. And it's better than a bike because I'm not hot when I arrive at work.
R: Where do you leave your scooter at work?
C: I take it into my office and I leave it near my desk.

R: Really?
C: Yeah, it isn't a problem.
R: Is it tiring to ride?
C: Yes, it *is* quite tiring. You can't really relax.
R: Is there anything else you don't like about the scooter?
C: Sometimes people laugh at me and I feel quite stupid. Oh yes, and people often stop me and ask questions about it! I don't like that.

UNIT 9   Recording 3

A: Oh, hi. I'm really sorry I'm late. I missed the train.
B: Hmm … I don't believe you.
A: No, really. The traffic was terrible.
B: And?
A: And my car broke down.
B: Your car, again?
A: And I left my wallet at home.
B: Ah, your wallet.
A: And … OK, I forgot about our meeting! I feel terrible about this.
B: Well, don't worry about it.
A: I'm so sorry.
B: No, really, it's fine.
A: I'm so, so …
B: That's OK! But don't let it happen again.

REVIEW 3   Recording 1

G = Greg   J = Jurgen

G: Hey, Jurgen. It's my wife's birthday tomorrow. Can you recommend a good restaurant?
J: Well, what kind of food do you like?
G: We both like Chinese food and, er, French food.
J: There's a good restaurant called Bouchon in town. It serves French food.
G: Do you think my wife would like it?
J: Yes, I think so. It's quite romantic.
G: Where is it?
J: It's in a small street near the cinema.
G: Can you tell me the way?
J: From the cinema, you go down Hillside Road past the pharmacy and turn left.
G: Left at the pharmacy. OK …
J: Then go straight on for about two hundred metres – Bouchon is on the right. It isn't far.
G: Great – thanks!
…
J: Hi, Greg. Did you find the restaurant?
G: No!
J: Oh? Why?
G: Your directions were all wrong! You said to turn *left* at the pharmacy.
J: Oh, no!
G: And we did, but it took us completely the wrong way!

J: Oh, no – I'm so sorry. I always mix up left and right.

G: Hm. My wife was really angry.

J: I feel terrible about this.

G: In the end we went home and ordered pizza!

J: Oh, no!

G: Ah, well. Maybe next year! Don't worry about it, really.

UNIT 10 Recording 1

hot, thirsty, warm, wet, lost, stung, cold, hungry

UNIT 10 Recording 2

1 Well, the most difficult thing was that there was so much water, but I was so thirsty. Food wasn't a big problem because I caught fish and ate them. Of course, I got sunburnt after the first day because I had nothing to put on my head. And I was afraid of sharks. Once I saw one, but it just swam around the raft for a few minutes and then it went away.

2 I felt very small and very tired. I walked all night, very slowly because of the sand, and I tried to stay cool in the daytime, but it was so hot. On the second day I found some water – that was very lucky – but then I wanted to walk more, not just stay by the water. I wanted to try to find my way back to the town. I had food with me, so I didn't get hungry – just very thirsty. Once I saw a snake and I was afraid that one might go into my shoe, so I never took my shoes off.

3 There was snow everywhere, everything was white, and that's why I got lost – I didn't see the path. I was up there only one night, but it was the longest night of my life. The most important thing was staying warm. I didn't have enough clothes with me, so I got terribly cold. I wanted to make a fire, but everything was wet. I slept on the ground and got colder. I didn't think about food – I wasn't really hungry, but just so thirsty! It was difficult, very difficult.

4 There was water, so I didn't get thirsty. And I didn't get too hungry because I knew what kind of plants to eat. Of course, I got very lost – I walked day and night – but you know, you can never, ever get bored there. There are so many different types of plants and animals and insects – it was beautiful. So yes, I felt tired and lost, but not bored.

UNIT 10 Recording 3

1 You get cold.
   You'll get cold.
2 We'll miss the train.
   We miss the train.
3 I'm sure you'll hate it.
   I'm sure you hate it.
4 They know you're a tourist.
   They'll know you're a tourist.
5 I stay at home.
   I'll stay at home.
6 I'll never go out.
   I never go out.

UNIT 11 Recording 1

elbow, thumb, leg, knee, head, neck, stomach, hand, nose, toe, mouth, back

UNIT 11 Recording 2

P = Presenter E = Emma

P: Hello and welcome to *Working Week*, where we take a look at the world of work. This week we're looking at time management. We all know there are twenty-four hours in a day, but some people are just much better at using these than other people. In today's programme we'll look at ways to improve the time we spend at work – things we should do and things we shouldn't. Professor Emma Fields from the Institute of Work Psychology joins us today. Emma, what are the good and bad time management techniques?

E: Well, the first thing you have to do is to make sure you have time to plan. Most of us start work without organising our week and days first. You should always give yourself some planning time. Secondly, make sure you don't forget your plans – write a to-do list for the day and for the week. We all try to keep too much in our heads and, of course, we forget things. It's better to make a list and make only one list – some people make two or three different lists and that doesn't help. Thirdly, put the most important things at the top of the list and do them first. A lot of people do the things they like doing first, not the important things. Fourthly, don't multi-task – do one thing, then do another thing. When you multi-task, you work more slowly – each task takes more time. And you often make mistakes when you do two or more things at the same time. Finally, work smarter, not harder. We all spend extra time in the office trying to finish something. But is that last hour on Friday the best time to do it? When you are tired and not concentrating? If you're smart, you'll make time for the task on Monday morning – you'll do it better and more quickly then.

UNIT 11 Recording 3

A: Are you OK, Jim?

B: No. I have to meet Anne at 5.30 and look at this list!

A: Let me help. I'm not busy at the moment.

B: Oh, can you? Thanks!

A: No problem. Shall I phone Noriko?

B: Yes, please.

A: And then I'll email the Moscow office.

B: Can you tell them I'll phone tomorrow?

A: OK. And I'll get some flowers for Ellie. I'm going to the hospital to see her tonight anyway.

B: Fantastic! Let me give you the money.

A: It's OK. Give it to me tomorrow.

B: Thanks a lot. I'll do the same for you any time!

UNIT 12 Recording 1

be in a play, ride an elephant, climb Mount Bromo, do a bungee jump, meet a new friend, go to a match, sleep outside, watch the sun rise

UNIT 12 Recording 2

1
A: Have you ever flown in a helicopter?

B: No, I haven't. Have you?

A: Yes, I have. Just once, when I went helicopter skiing – five years ago.

B: That sounds interesting. What's helicopter skiing?

A: A helicopter takes you up the mountain and you ski from there.

B: And how was it?

A: It was fun. I enjoyed it.

2
A: Matt, have you ever sung in a karaoke club?

B: No, but I've sung at a party. It was last year sometime. No, two years ago. At a birthday party.

A: What did you sing?

B: I can't remember … Oh, yes – *I did it my way*. It was fun. I can't sing, but it was a good laugh. Why are you asking?

A: I'm going to a karaoke club tonight and I'm feeling quite nervous about it.

B: You'll be all right. Just relax and enjoy it!

3
A: What's the matter?

B: I have to drive to Dublin tomorrow and look at the rain! Have you ever driven in really bad weather?

A: Yes. I drove up to Scotland to visit my grandparents in 2007 and it just snowed non-stop – it was impossible to see the road ahead.

B: Sounds dangerous.

A: Yes, so I stopped and stayed overnight in a hotel. After that I always visit them by train!

B: Yeah, that's a good idea. Maybe I'll go by train.

4

A: Look at this picture. It looks scary! Have you ever been on a roller coaster like that?

B: Yes, when I was about nineteen, in Munich. A friend of mine took me on a really big roller coaster.

A: Were you afraid?

B: No. After ten seconds I closed my eyes and didn't open them until it stopped!

UNIT 12   Recording 3

1 three two three, four double nine six
2 six double eight, two nine seven five
3 oh seven five, seven two eight one
4 six two three, two double eight nine
5 nine eight nine, double seven double six
6 oh eight seven oh, five double three, eight double nine two

REVIEW 4   Recording 1

A: Could I speak to Susie Dee?

B: She's not at home. She's back at three. Could you phone her back tonight?

A: I'll leave a message. Is that all right?

B: Just a moment, I need a pen.

A: She's got my number. My name's Ben.

B: Let me check … your name is Jack?

A: Oh, never mind – I'll call her back.

A: Well, hello Susie! How are you?

C: I'm fine. What would you like to do?

A: Why don't we meet and have a chat?

C: I don't really feel like doing that.

A: Then how about a walk together?

C: Sounds good. Let me check the weather.
It's going to rain – that's not ideal.

A: So let's stay in and cook a meal!

Pearson Education Limited
Edinburgh Gate
Harlow
Essex CM20 2JE
England
and Associated Companies throughout the world.

www.pearsonelt.com

First published 2015
9th impression 2022
ISBN: 978-1-2921-1430-9

Set in Aptifer sans 10/12 pt
Printed in Slovakia by Neografia

Photo acknowledgements
The publisher would like to thank the following for their kind permission to reproduce their photographs:

(Key: b-bottom; c-centre; l-left; r-right; t-top)

123RF.com: Graça Victoria 53 (E), 27/3, 27/8, 28 (Apple), 28 (Cheese), 28 (Chicken), 28 (Milk), 28 (Orange Juice), 28 (Pear), 43/1, 43/2, 43/3, Stefano Cavoretto 27/4, djem 53 (H), Jennifer Keddie de Cojon 10, Maksym Yemelyanov 27/7; **Alamy Images:** Robert Fried 32t, Hangon Media Works Private limited 18b, Horizons WWP 74, International Photobank 42, Natalie Jezzard 56, MBI 60, Rory Buckland L 24, Robin Weaver 52; **Fotolia.com:** cristi180884 48/3, eugenesergeev 53 (B), fotomatrix 48/8 (Blouse), Brent Hofacker 31, julialine802 43/7, Alexandra Karamyshev 48/1, 48/4, 48/5, larisa13 6b, OlegDoroshin 48/9, Popova Olga 48/10, Kimberly Reinick 27/1, sugar0607 6tl, Martin Turzak 6tc, underworld 53 (C), Lilyana Vynogradova 6tr, WavebreakMediaMicro 16, zakaz 48/7; **Getty Images:** Ghislain & Marie David de Lossy / The Image Bank 54, Ian Cook / The LIFE Images Collection 35, Jupiterimages 65, Mark Bowden / Vetta 15, SD Productions / Photodisc 36, Stephen Mallon / The Image Bank 12, Stone / Michelle Pedone 41; **Pearson Education Ltd:** Gareth Boden 32b, MindStudio 44; **Rex Features:** Action Press 34t, Erik C. Pendzich 34b; **Shutterstock.com:** 6493866629 28 (Bread), Andresr 19t, bikeriderlondon 63, Binkski 53 (F), BlueOrange Studio 43/6, Bola_BR 28 (Garlic), chikapylka 28 (Pepper), Djomas 48 (E), Elena Elisseeva 53 (I), Freer 28 (Potato), Goodluz 59r, Peter Gudella 27/10, Anton Gvozdikov 66b, Jiri Hera 27/6, Hogan Imaging 48 (J), terekhov igor 48/8, IR Stone 25, Juniart 48 (D), Kaarsten 48 (G), Karkas 48/2, 48/6 (Jacket), KKulikov 27/2, Robert Kneschke 66t, Kuzma 28 (Strawberry), wong yu liang 48 (I), Oleksiy Mark 53 (G), Maxriesgo 48 (B), 48 (C), michaeljung 48 (A), motorolka 28 (Broccoli), Maks Narodenko 28 (Banana), nickichen 43/4, Pablo Eder 27/5, Pkchai 59c, Elena Schweitzer 28 (Butter), Shebeko 48/3 (Jumper), Shout It Out Design 53 (D), Somchai Som 43/8, Alex Staroseltsev 28 (Salmon), Alexey Stiop 43/9, Stockyimages 48 (H), Studioloco 48 (F), Surrphoto 49, Thaagoon 27/9, Vibrant Image Studio 53 (A), violetblue 59l, Vladimir Wrangel 43/5; **SuperStock:** Blend Images 20, Radius 62

All other images © Pearson Education

Every effort has been made to trace the copyright holders and we apologise in advance for any unintentional omissions. We would be pleased to insert the appropriate acknowledgement in any subsequent edition of this publication.